Volume
2

HMS SERIES HISTORY MADE SIMPLE

THE WEIMAR REPUBLIC
AND
THE RISE OF THE
NAZIS
1919-1933

KURT E. BREITNER

The following book, originally released in electro[...] compiled for paperback publishing to the best of our [...] original illustration quality and complex formatting of t[...] successive pages are the unaltered manuscript.

A Premier Publishing Service
Serving Corporations, Academic Institutions, Business Professionals, Organizations and Individuals

ISBN: 978-1499709384

Published in the United States of America

First Edition – English
eReader Release: February 2014 - New York, NY.
Paperback Release: May 2014 - Dearborn, MI.
Illustrations by: Lefteris Vagenas

DEDICATION

TO ALL THOSE WHO EVER TOOK A HISTORY BOOK DOWN FROM A SHELF AND READ IT FROM COVER TO COVER, AND - ESPECIALLY - TO ALL THOSE WHO NEVER HAVE.

PREFACE...

THIS VOLUME ON THE WEIMAR REPUBLIC AND THE RISE OF THE NAZIS IS THE SECOND IN THE FOUR-VOLUME HISTORY MADE SIMPLE SERIES (HMSS) ON GERMANY. THE OTHER VOLUMES ARE *THE GERMAN EMPIRE (1871-1918), NAZI GERMANY (1933-1945)*, AND, *POST-WAR GERMANY: FROM DIVISION TO REUNIFICATION (1945-PRESENT)*.

HMSS BOOKS ARE FOR EVERYONE WHO FINDS HISTORY DULL AND BORING. LET'S FACE IT, MOST OF US AREN'T HISTORY BUFFS. WE DON'T SPEND OUR FREE TIME READING UP ON HISTORICAL PERIODS, PERSONS, OR EVENTS. WE'D SOONER SURF THE WEB OR VEGETATE ON A COUCH WITH A REMOTE CONTROL THAN READ THE TYPICAL HISTORY BOOK.

HMSS OFFERS A NEW APPROACH TO TRANSMITTING HISTORICAL INFORMATION. IT MAKES THE HISTORY OF SEPARATE COUNTRIES AS SIMPLE AND ENJOYABLE AS POSSIBLE WITH HUNDREDS OF ILLUSTRATIONS, AND LOTS OF HUMOR AND IRONY - JUST THE INGREDIENTS THAT MAKE LIFE ITSELF INTERESTING.

ALL HISTORICAL ACTORS, LARGE AND SMALL, VOICE THEIR OPINIONS AND ARGUE WITH EACH OTHER - AND SOMETIMES WITH ME, THE AUTHOR. HISTORY CAN'T BE INTERESTING TO THE NON-SPECIALIST WHEN IT'S SERVED UP AS A COLD MONOLOGUE LIKE THE NINE O'CLOCK NEWS.

YOU MIGHT SAY HISTORY'S A FUTILE EXERCISE. WE CAN'T AGREE ABOUT THE PRESENT, HOW CAN WE POSSIBLY AGREE ABOUT THE PAST, RIGHT? SURE, BUT WHO SAID WE HAVE TO AGREE ABOUT EVERYTHING? AND AREN'T THE MOST INFORMED OPINIONS ALL SIDES OF AN ARGUMENT?

...ANYWAY, I'VE PROBABLY SAID ENOUGH, OR TOO MUCH. SO SIT BACK, MAKE YOURSELF COMFORTABLE, AND ENJOY THE READ!

Kurt E. Breitner

ACKNOWLEDGMENT

I SHOULD LIKE TO THANK EVERYONE WHO PROVIDED ADVICE DURING THE CONCEPTUALIZATION, RESEARCH AND WRITING OF THIS BOOK. YOU KNOW WHO YOU ARE AND I AM GRATEFUL TO YOU. THE HMSS PROJECT WOULD NEVER HAVE GOTTEN OFF THE GROUND WITHOUT THE IMAGINATIVE SKETCHES OF LEFTERIS VAGENAS AND THE TECHNICAL AND ORGANIZATIONAL SUPPORT OF NICK POURNARAS. I AM ALSO GREATLY INDEBTED TO PROFESSORS DANIEL MULHOLLAND OF TUFTS UNIVERSITY AND ROBERT BRYM OF THE UNIVERSITY OF TORONTO FOR THEIR GENEROUS AND INSIGHTFUL COMMENTS ON HOW TO IMPROVE THE MANUSCRIPT.

GERMANY ATTACKED FRANCE IN AUGUST OF 1914 AND SET OFF WORLD WAR ONE. FOUR YEARS AND THREE MONTHS LATER, IN OCTOBER 1918, THE GERMAN ARMY WAS STILL IN FRANCE, BUT IN FULL RETREAT. THE *REIICHSWEHR* WAS STEADILY BEING PUSHED BACK BY FRENCH, BRITISH AND AMERICAN TROOPS, AMONG OTHERS.

THEN, ON OCTOBER 28, 1918, REBELLION BROKE OUT AT THE GERMAN NAVY'S BASES OF **WILHELMSHAVEN** AND **KIEL** ON THE BALTIC SEA COAST. REBELLION ISN'T AN EVERYDAY EVENT, ESPECIALLY AMONG MILITARY PERSONNEL. WHY DID IT HAPPEN?

If our aristocrat officers want to commit suicide, that's fire, but we sure won't!

THE SAILORS REFUSED TO BOARD THEIR SHIPS AND TAKE PART IN ONE LAST BATTLE FOR THE "HONOR" OF THE GERMAN NAVY. INSTEAD, THEY **MUTINIED.**

THIS SET IN MOTION A SERIES OF EVENTS THAT LED TO THE GERMAN REVOLUTION, WHICH SPREAD THROUGHOUT MUCH OF THE COUNTRY OVER THE NEXT WEEK.

We no longer take orders from our officers, and we listen only to our Council!

SAILORS, SOLDIERS AND WORKERS BEGAN ELECTING **COUNCILS** (*SOLDATEN UND ARBEITERRÄTE*). (A COUNCIL IS A GROUP THAT'S FORMED TO DEAL WITH PROBLEMS.)

THE COUNCILS WANTED THE END OF GERMANY'S MONARCHY AND FOR *KAISER* WILHELM II TO STEP DOWN. (HERE I OUGHT TO EXPLAIN THAT THE GERMAN WORD *KAISER* COMES FROM THE LATIN "CAESAR" AND MEANS "EMPEROR"; AND A MONARCHY IS A SYSTEM OF GOVERNMENT IN WHICH POLITICAL POWER IS HELD BY ONE PERSON, THE MONARCH. THE WORD COMES FROM THE GREEK "*MONO*" OR "SOLE", AND "*ARCHY*" OR "RULE"; IT MEANS THE RULE OF ONE PERSON.)

APART FROM WANTING GERMANY TO BECOME A DEMOCRACY (A SYSTEM OF GOVERNMENT WHERE POLITICAL POWER IS HELD BY THE PEOPLE), MOST OF THE GERMAN *SOLDATEN UND ARBEITER-RÄTE* ALSO WANTED SOCIALISM. IN OTHER WORDS, THEY WANTED TO ELIMINATE THE PRIVILEGES OF THE COUNTRY'S UPPER CLASSES, THE LANDED ARISTOCRATS, WHO WERE KNOWN AS *JUNKERS*, AND THE BIG INDUSTRIALISTS. SOME OF THE MORE RADICAL COUNCILS WANTED TO DO AWAY WITH CAPITALISM AND BUILD A SOCIETY WITHOUT PRIVATE PROPERTY AND RICH AND POOR CLASSES.

MEMBERS OF THE UPPER CLASSES (PEOPLE WITH A LOT OF LAND OR MONEY, LIKE THE GUY ON THE RIGHT) WERE TERRIFIED OF THE COUNCILS AS THE REVOLUTION SPREAD AND THE *RÄTE* SEIZED POWER IN VARIOUS CITIES. THIS WAS ACHIEVED IN MOST PLACES PEACEFULLY AND WITHOUT LOSS OF LIFE.
This is terrible! The councils'll copy what the Soviets did in Russia. The last thing we need here in Germany is socialism!

THE STRONGEST POLITICAL PARTY IN GERMANY AT THE TIME WAS THE **SOCIAL DEMOCRATIC PARTY (S.P.D).** IT WAS DIVIDED INTO TWO MAJOR FACTIONS.

ONE FACTION, THE **INDEPENDENT SOCIAL DEMOCRATS (U.S.P.D),** CALLED FOR IMMEDIATE PEACE NEGOTIATIONS TO END THE WAR AND WANTED SOCIALISM BASED ON THE COUNCILS.

THE OTHER FACTION WAS THE REMAINING MAJORITY IN THE **S.P.D,** WHICH WAS LED BY A MAN CALLED **FRIEDRICH EBERT.**

EBERT WASN'T VERY RADICAL AND DIDN'T WANT GERMANY TO HAVE A SOCIALIST REVOLUTION. HE PREFERRED TO KEEP THE GERMAN MONARCHY, BUT WITH A DIFFERENT RULER THAN *KAISER* WILHELM II.

UNFORTUNATELY FOR EBERT AND HIS PARTY (THE S.P.D), SOCIALIST REVOLUTION SEEMED MORE LIKELY WITH THE PASSING OF EACH DAY.

If the *Kaiser* doesn't step down, the revolution is inevitable. But I don't want it, I even hate it like **sin**!
SPD leader Friedrich Ebert

ON NOVEMBER 7, 1918, THE REVOLUTION REACHED THE CITY OF MUNICH, THE CAPITAL OF THE LARGE SOUTHERN GERMAN STATE OF BAVARIA, AND KING LUDWIG III WAS FORCED TO FLEE. (GERMANY, AS WE SAW IN BOOK ONE, *THE GERMAN EMPIRE, 1871-1918*, HAD A FEDERAL STRUCTURE WITH NUMEROUS STATES, EACH WITH ITS OWN RULER; THE "TOP RULER" WAS *KAISER* WILHELM II.)

King Ludwig III of Bavaria (before he fled).

A SOCIALIST GOVERNMENT WAS PROCLAIMED IN BAVARIA UNDER THE LEADERSHIP OF ACTOR AND RADICAL SOCIALIST, KURT EISNER.

Bavaria now has a government **of** the people **for** the people!

Kurt Eisner

WHAT EISNER MEANT WAS THAT THE KING WOULD NO LONGER RULE BAVARIA. BAVARIA WAS NOW SOCIALIST AND SIMPLE WORKING PEOPLE WOULD RULE BY AND FOR THEMSELVES.

TWO DAYS LATER, ON NOVEMBER 9, 1918, GERMANY'S LIBERAL-MINDED CHANCELLOR (THE WORD THE GERMANS USE FOR PRIME MINISTER), **PRINCE MAX VON BADEN**, DID SOMETHING QUITE UNUSUAL: HE LIED TO EVERYONE AND SAID THAT *KAISER* WILHELM II HAD GIVEN UP HIS THRONE - THAT HE'D ABDICATED!

Today, the *Kaiser* abdicated. Oh, and I'm resigning as well.

THE GOOD PRINCE HANDED HIS POSITION OVER TO S.P.D LEADER **FRIEDRICH EBERT**, WHO NOW BECAME GERMANY'S NEW CHANCELLOR.

My first action as Chancellor is to ask the people to remain calm, get off the streets, and to restore peace and order!
Friedrich Ebert

THIS DIDN'T WORK....

....A LITTLE LATER ON THE SAME DAY (NOVEMBER 9, 1918), EBERT DECIDED TO HAVE LUNCH.

HE DINED IN THE *REICHSTAG*, OR PARLIAMENT BUILDING, TOGETHER WITH ANOTHER LEADER OF THE SOCIAL DEMOCRATIC PARTY, A MAN CALLED **PHILIPP SCHEIDEMANN.**

WHILE THE TWO MEN WERE EATING, MASSES OF PEOPLE GATHERED OUTSIDE THE BUILDING, AND WANTED EBERT TO TALK TO THEM...

...FOR SOME REASON, EBERT REFUSED.

NOW SHEIDEMANN SEIZED THE OPPORTUNITY TO GO OUT ONTO A BALCONY, DECLARE THE END OF THE MONARCHY AND PROCLAIM THE BIRTH OF THE GERMAN REPUBLIC.

The monarchy is *kaput!* Long live the German Republic!

Philipp Scheidemann announcing the end of the German Empire.

EBERT WAS **FURIOUS!**

EBERT WANTED THE DECISION TO TURN GERMANY FROM A MONARCHY INTO A DEMOCRACY TO BE MADE BY AN ELECTED NATIONAL ASSEMBLY, OR PARLIAMENT - EVEN IF IT DECIDED TO BRING BACK THE MONARCHY.

You have no right to proclaim the Republic!
Too late now!
Scheidemann
Ebert

SINCE *KAISER* WILHELM II HADN'T ACTUALLY ABDICATED ON NOVEMBER 9, 1918, GERMANY OFFICIALLY REMAINED A MONARCHY UNTIL HE SIGNED THE DOCUMENT THAT SAID HE WAS STEPPING DOWN FROM THE THRONE ON NOVEMBER 28, 1918. THE *KAISER* DID THIS FROM HOLLAND, WHERE HE'D FLED ON NOVEMBER 10 - THE DAY AFTER SCHEIDEMANN MADE HIS FAMOUS DECLARATION.

EBERT NOW GOT THE AGREEMENT OF THE INDEPENDENT SOCIALISTS (U.S.P.D) TO COOPERATE IN THE SAME GOVERNMENT WITH HIS SOCIAL DEMOCRATIC PARTY (S.P.D). HE REALLY DIDN'T LIKE COOPERATING WITH PEOPLE WHO WERE MORE RADICAL THAN HIMSELF, BUT BEING CLEVER, HE KNEW THERE WAS NO OTHER WAY TO INFLUENCE THE SITUATION THE WAY HE WANTED.

IN THEORY, THIS NEW GOVERNMENT REPRESENTED THE SOLDIERS' AND WORKERS' COUNCILS. REFLECTING THE RADICAL SPIRIT OF THE TIMES, IT WAS CALLED *RAT DER VOLKSBEAUFTRAGTEN* OR "COUNCIL OF PEOPLE'S COMMISSIONERS" (A COMMISSIONER IS SOMEONE WHO'S BEEN GIVEN THE POWER TO ACT BY A COMMISION, AND IS AN OFFICIAL OF A PUBLIC SERVICE).

What a situation I'm in! The SPD's in power and we can pass laws to improve the lives of the working people. But because of the revolution, I must share power with people further to the left - the Independent Socialists and other crazies!

Ebert in his office.

Ebert's clever. He now has the cooperation of the USPD and the Councils. Since he's the head of the government, he'll lead the revolution in the direction he wants.

Ebert's direction *wasn't* revolutionary!

DEMOCRATIC GOVERNMENT IN GERMANY WAS BORN IN VERY DIFFICULT CIRCUMSTANCES. THE WAR EFFORT HAD COLLAPSED, THE *KAISER* HAD ABDICATED, THE FLEET WAS IN MUTINY AT WILHELMSHAVEN AND KIEL, AND SOLDIERS' AND WORKERS' COUNCILS HAD APPEARED IN BERLIN, COLOGNE AND MUNICH (AND HERE A SOCIALIST GOVERNMENT WAS IN CHARGE).

THE DEMOCRATIC GOVERNMENT THAT AROSE IN GERMANY FROM THE ASHES OF WORLD WAR ONE WAS AN ARTIFICIAL REGIME - IT HADN'T BEEN ELECTED BY THE GERMAN PEOPLE.

THIS IS WHAT EBERT HAD TO SAY ABOUT THE MATTER.
So what? There was no time for elections. The SPD's the biggest party in parliament and our government has roots in the long traditions of German social democracy that go way back to 1848!

THE REALITY WAS THAT EBERT AND HIS SOCIAL DEMOCRATIC PARTY WERE RUSHED INTO POWER BY THE COUNTRY'S TOP GENERALS.

GERMANY'S MILITARY LEADERS REPRESENTED THE ARISTOCRATIC LANDED ELITE OF THE COUNTRY, THE *JUNKERS*. THESE PEOPLE ABANDONED THE *KAISER* BECAUSE THEY SAW THAT WILHELM II COULD NO LONGER GUARANTEE THEIR INTERESTS.

The *Junkers* expected the peace terms of the French, British, and Americans would reflect the even nature of WWI.

GENERALS PAUL VON HINDENBURG AND ERICH LUDENDORFF DECIDED THAT THE BEST THING TO DO WAS TO STOP THE GREAT WAR PREMATURELY AND CALL IT A DRAW.

THEY DID THIS BECAUSE THEY KNEW THAT LETTING THE WAR PLAY OUT MEANT THE ANNIHILATION OF THE GERMAN ARMY AND TOTAL DEFEAT. IT ALSO MEANT A GERMANY IN WHICH THE *JUNKERS* WOULD NO LONGER HAVE THEIR TRADITIONAL ROLE AS RULERS AND PRIVILEGED ELITE.

A lot was at stake. We *Junkers* had to look out for number one.

AFTER THE MONARCHY WAS ABOLISHED AND THE REPUBLIC PROCLAIMED IN NOVEMBER OF 1918, GERMANY'S FLAG WAS CHANGED. THE BLACK-RED-WHITE FLAG OF THE EMPIRE WAS REPLACED BY A BLACK-RED-GOLD *(SCHWARZ-ROT-GOLD)* FLAG - THE COLORS OF THE LIBERAL NATIONAL ASSEMBLY IN FRANKFURT DURING THE FAILED REVOLUTION OF 1848.

The young Republic wanted to say with the new flag that its origin was in the democratic political movement that had swept Germany back in 1848.

ANTI-REPUBLICAN
We oppose the new FLAG

BUT MANY PEOPLE IN GERMANY WEREN'T HAPPY WITH THE NEW GOVERNMENT AND ITS FLAG.

GERMANY'S NAVY, OR *REICHSMARINE*, FOR EXAMPLE, INSISTED ON USING THE PRE-1918 BLACK, RED AND WHITE COLORS OF THE *KAISERLICHE MARINE*, THE *KAISER'S* NAVY. SO DID THE COUNTRY'S MERCHANT MARINE.

DESPITE ITS NEW DEMOCRATIC POLITICAL FORM, THE NEW REPUBLIC WAS STILL KNOWN AS THE *DEUTSCHES REICH*. THIS PHRASE IS OFTEN TRANSLATED INTO ENGLISH AS "GERMAN EMPIRE". HOWEVER, SINCE THE GERMAN WORD *REICH* HAS MORE MEANINGS THAN THE ENGLISH WORD "EMPIRE" (THE WORD "REALM" IS CLOSER IN MEANING), MOST HISTORIANS DON'T TRANSLATE THE WORD AND SIMPLY SAY "GERMAN *REICH*".

BUT LET'S RETURN TO EBERT AND THE SOCIAL DEMOCRATS...

THE SOCIAL DEMOCRATIC PARTY FOUND ITSELF CATAPULTED INTO POWER WITH HUGE HANDICAPS THAT WOULD HAUNT THE WEIMAR REPUBIC IN THE FUTURE.

WE'LL SOON SEE THAT THE FIRST HANDICAP OF THE WEIMAR REPUBLIC...

Weimar? Why did it have such a weird name?

Weimar was the name of the small town where the National Assembly adopted the new constitution. There was too much anarchy and chaos in Berlin...all kinds of armed men roamed the streets.

...WAS THE SHARE OF RESPONSIBILITY THE S.P.D LEADERS HAD FOR SIGNING THE **TREATY OF VERSAILLES** ON JUNE 28, 1919, WITH THE VICTORS OF WORLD WAR ONE - FRANCE, BRITAIN, ITALY, AND THE UNITED STATES OF AMERICA. MANY GERMANS TRULY BELIEVED THAT THE TREATY WAS WAY TOO TOUGH AND COMPLETELY UNFAIR!

THE DATE FOR THE SIGNING WAS CHOSEN ON PURPOSE, JUNE 28, TO COMMEMORATE THE DAY ARCHDUKE FRANZ FERDINAND, THE HEIR TO THE THRONE OF THE AUSTRO-HUNGARIAN EMPIRE, WAS MURDERED IN SARAJEVO, BOSNIA, IN 1914 - THE SPARK THAT HAD SET OFF THE GREATEST WAR THE WORLD HAD YET TO SEE.

The peace terms were presented to the Germans by these four men, Italy's Vittorio Orlando, Britain's David Lloyd-George, France's Georges Clemenceau and the USA's Woodrow Wilson.

If the Treaty of Versailles was so unfair, why did Germany's traditional elite accept it? Why didn't they put the army on a war footing again, take over Ebert's government in Berlin, and tell the Allies to get lost?
That was impossible! The Allies would've immediately occupied the country. And the political instability in Germany might've blown into a full-scale civil war.
JUNKER

WE'LL SEE THAT PROBABLY THE MOST IMPORTANT FACTOR LEADING TO THE NASTY PHENOMENA OF HITLER AND NAZISM WAS THE EXTREMELY NEGATIVE REACTION OF GERMANY'S CONSERVATIVE UPPER CLASSES TO THE PUNISHMENT THAT THE TREATY OF VERSAILLES HANDED THE COUNTRY...

...AND SINCE THEY NEEDED SOMEONE TO BLAME FOR GERMANY'S HUMILIATION AND THE END OF THE MONARCHY, THEY BLAMED THE SO-CALLED "**NOVEMBER CRIMINALS**" - THE NAME THEY GAVE TO THE PEOPLE WHO'D SIGNED THE ARMIISTICE THAT ENDED THE GREAT WAR ON NOVEMBER 11, 1918.

Deutsche.
denKt daran!

THIS WAS THE ***DOLCHSTOSSLEGENDE*** OR "STAB-IN-THE-BACK" MYTH. A VERY SIMPLE THEORY, IT WAS FIRST PUT FORWARD BY GERMANY'S GENERALS, AND WENT SOMETHING LIKE THIS: "TRAITORS" - SOCIALISTS AND JEWS - SIGNED THE ARMISTICE DESPITE THE FACT THAT NO FOREIGN SOLDIERS HAD SET FOOT ON GERMAN SOIL. THE GERMAN ARMY COULD VE STILL WON THE WAR BECAUSE IT WAS IN FRANCE (AND RUSSIA), AND HADN'T BEEN DEFEATED ON THE BATTLEFIELD. INSTEAD, WENT THE MYTH, THE ARMY HAD BEEN STABBED IN THE BACK BY TRAITORS!

Why did these people blame the Jews? What did Jews have to do with the Armistice?
Nothing. But because of other indirect factors, the Jews were blamed. For example, there were a few Jews among the leaders of the Soviet Union, and Kurt Eisner, who led the Bavarian Socialist Republic, was a Jew who'd been writing since 1916 about the illegal nature of WWI.
I AM FROM TODAY

ANTI-SEMITISM WAS A REALITY IN GERMANY, AS IT WAS IN MANY COUNTRIES IN EUROPE. LIKE RACISM IN GENERAL, THE STAB-IN-THE-BACK THEORY WASN'T TO BE TOPPLED BY LOGIC.

THE FACT REMAINS (AND FACTS ARE VERY STUBBORN THINGS) THAT WHEN THE WAR WAS STOPPED, THE GERMAN ARMY WAS IN FULL RETREAT ALONG THE ENTIRE WESTERN FRONT, IT HAD SUFFERED DEFEAT AFTER DEFEAT, FRESH AMERICAN TROOPS KEPT ARRIVING IN FRANCE TO MAKE THE ALLIES INCREASINGLY STRONGER, THERE WAS DISCONTENT, HUNGER, AND UNREST IN GERMANY, AND THE NAVY WAS IN MUTINY.

No way could Germany've won the War. This stab-in-the-back theory sounds like sour grapes to me! I wonder how the fanatics responded to these bare facts?
How else? They said that despite the fantastic odds, Germany would've won the war if it had been allowed to continue.
I AM FROM TODAY

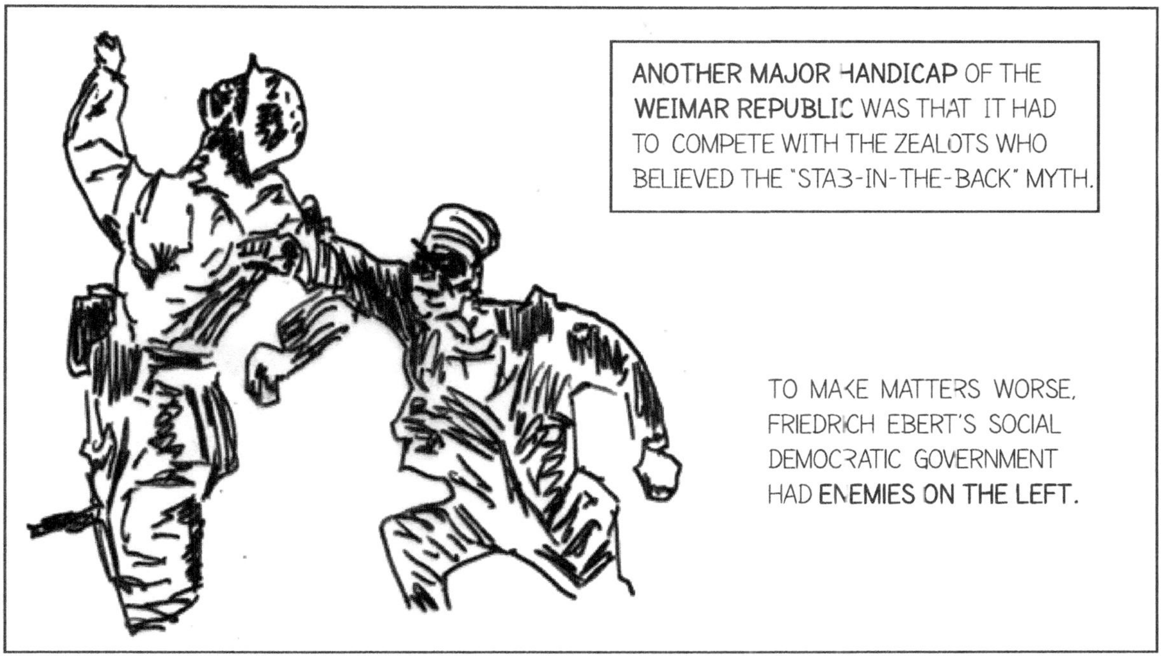
ANOTHER MAJOR HANDICAP OF THE WEIMAR REPUBLIC WAS THAT IT HAD TO COMPETE WITH THE ZEALOTS WHO BELIEVED THE "STAB-IN-THE-BACK" MYTH.
TO MAKE MATTERS WORSE, FRIEDRICH EBERT'S SOCIAL DEMOCRATIC GOVERNMENT HAD ENEMIES ON THE LEFT.

I don't quite get this. Wasn't the government democratic?
Yes, but the German democrats were deeply divided between the SPD and the far more radical USPD, or Independent Social Democratic Party.

AN EVEN MORE EXTREME LEFT-WING GROUP WAS FORMED IN 1918, THE *SPARTAKUS BUND* OR SPARTACIST UNION. THESE MARXIST REVOLUTIONARIES NAMED THEMSELVES AFTER THE ROMAN SLAVE REBEL, SPARTACUS. VERY SOON THEY'D ADOPT THE NAME **COMMUNIST PARTY OF GERMANY** OR ***KOMMUNISTISCHE PARTEI DEUTSCHLANDS*** **(K.P.D).**

THE COMMUNIST LEADERS WERE **KARL LIEBKNECHT** AND **ROSA LUXEMBURG.**

Workers of the world, *unite!*

Rasa Luxemburg haranguing a crowd.

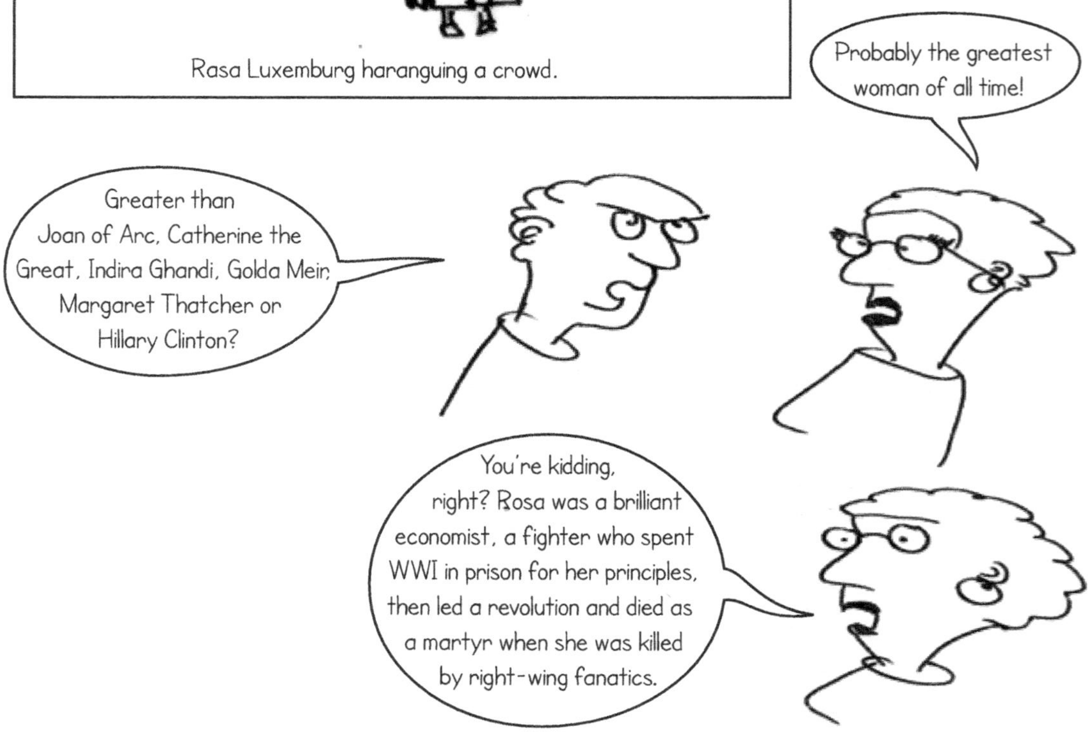
Probably the greatest woman of all time!
Greater than Joan of Arc, Catherine the Great, Indira Ghandi, Golda Meir, Margaret Thatcher or Hillary Clinton?
You're kidding, right? Rosa was a brilliant economist, a fighter who spent WWI in prison for her principles, then led a revolution and died as a martyr when she was killed by right-wing fanatics.

THE COMMUNISTS WANTED TO COME TO POWER AND CARRY OUT RADICAL PROGRAMS LIKE THE ONES LENIN'S BOLSHEVIKS HAD INTRODUCED IN RUSSIA. ULTIMATELY, THEY WANTED TO ABOLISH PRIVATE PROPERTY AND GET RID OF FREE MARKET CAPITALISM IN GERMANY.

THEY MADE THIS CRYSTAL CLEAR ON THE VERY DAY THE GERMAN *REICH* DIED ON NOVEMBER 9, 1918. JUST A FEW HOURS AFTER THE S.P.D's PHILIPP SCHEIDEMANN ANNOUNCED THE CREATION OF THE GERMAN REPUBLIC, **KARL LIEBKNECHT** OF THE *SPARTAKUSBUND* PROCLAIMED FROM ANOTHER BERLIN BALCONY THE CREATION OF A "FREE SOCIALIST REPUBLIC".

Karl Liebknecht on November 9, 1918.

FROM NOVEMBER 1918 TO JANUARY 1919, GERMANY WAS GOVERNED BY THE COUNCIL OF PEOPLE'S COMMISSIONERS UNDER THE LEADERSHIP OF FRIEDRICH EBERT AND HUGO HAASE (HE WAS THE HEAD OF THE INDEPENDENT SOCIALISTS, THE U.S.P.D).

MANY **NEW LAWS** WERE INTRODUCED THAT RADICALLY SHIFTED GERMAN POLICIES TO THE LEFT. THESE INCLUDED THE 8-HOUR WORKDAY, DOMESTIC LABOR REFORM, AGRICULTURAL LABOR REFORM, PROTECTION FROM ARBITRARY DISMISSAL, AND, LAST BUT NOT LEAST, UNIVERSAL SUFFRAGE, WHICH MEANT THAT BOTH MEN AND WOMEN IN GERMANY WHO WERE 21 OR OLDER COULD NOW VOTE IN ALL TYPES OF ELECTIONS, BOTH LOCAL AND NATIONAL.

German women now got the right to vote!

UNLIKE THE COMMUNISTS, THE SOCIAL DEMOCRATS PREFERRED DEMOCRATIC AND PEACEFUL CHANGE. THE S.P.D DIDN'T HAVE THE STOMACH FOR THE KIND OF ARMED, RADICAL WORKING CLASS REVOLUTION THAT HAD TAKEN PLACE IN RUSSIA IN 1917.

The Communist Spartacists are fools! They actually believe that a socialist revolution is possible in Germany!

ACTUALLY, THE VIEW THAT RADICAL SOCIALIST REVOLUTION WASN'T A REALISTIC POSSIBILITY IN GERMANY IN 1918-19 IS PROBABLY CORRECT.

But objective conditions for revolution - capitalism, and thus a proletariat - exist in Germany!
Objective conditions aren't enough for a revolutionary situation!
GERMAN NAVY

What on Earth are they talking about?

THE MAIN DIFFERENCE BETWEEN THE REVOLUTIONARY POTENTIALS OF GERMANY AND RUSSIA WAS THAT IN GERMANY MOST PEASANTS OWNED THEIR LAND. THIS MEANT THAT THEY COULDN'T BE "NEUTRALIZED", AS THEY'D BEEN IN RUSSIA WHEN LENIN RETURNED FROM EXILE IN SWITZERLAND IN 1917 TO UTTER HIS SLOGAN "PEACE, BREAD, LAND".

By *peace* Lenin meant an immediate end to Russia's involvement in WWI.
RUSSIAN SOLDIER
Bread meant work.
RUSSIAN FACTORY WORKER
By *land* he meant we peasants could keep the land we seized from the noble landlords - Russia's *Junkers* - when we "voted with our feet", left the front, and went back to our villages.
RUSSIAN SOLDIER
But... that's theft!
Tell that to someone whose family were serfs laboring for free for the noble landlords for generations!
RUSSIAN SOLDIER

ENOUGH PEOPLE WERE GUNG-HO ENOUGH TO TRY AND MAKE A SOCIALIST REVOLUTION IN GERMANY. THE LEADERS OF THE COMMUNISTS, ROSA LUXEMBURG AND KARL LIEBKNECHT, WERE LESS SURE, AND DIDN'T RECOMMEND SUCH DRASTIC ACTION.

BLOODY FIGHTING BROKE OUT IN JANUARY 1919 IN THE STREETS OF BERLIN. ON ONE SIDE OF THE BARRICADES WERE GOVERNMENT TROOPS. ON THE OTHER WERE THE COMMUNISTS, TRADE UNIONISTS, SIMPLE PEOPLE AND THE RADICAL KIEL SAILORS OF THE *VOLKSMARINE DIVISION* WHO'D COME DOWN TO BERLIN IN TRUCKS AND TRAINS FROM THEIR KIEL AND WILHELMSHAVEN NAVAL BASES, TAKEN OVER THE *SCHLOSS*, OR PALACE, AS WELL AS THE THE OFFICES OF THE SOCIAL DEMOCRATIC PARTY'S NEWSPAPER, *VORWARTS* ("FORWARD").

Volksmarine

NONE OF THE REVOLUTIONARIES KNEW IT AT THE TIME, BUT THEIR JANUARY 1919 SPARTACIST UPRISING IN BERLIN WAS DOOMED TO TOTAL FAILURE.

Karl Radek

KARL RADEK, A TALENTED REVOLUTIONARY STRATEGIST AND MEMBER OF LENIN'S TEAM IN RUSSIA, WAS IN BERLIN AT THE TIME. HE WARNED THE SPARTACISTS THAT THE CORRELATION OF FORCES DIDN'T FAVOR THEIR CAUSE, AND BELIEVED GERMANY WASN'T READY FOR SOMETHING AS RADICAL AS SOCIALIST REVOLUTION.

Listen, if you try now you'll fail. You're not strong enough. The forces of reaction will rip you to pieces.
I know, but the party base insists.
There's no revolutionary situation in Berlin. Those who are ruled are no longer willing to be ruled, but those who rule are still able to rule!
Karl Radek
Rosa Luxemburg
Vlacimir Lenn

NONE OF THE COMMUNISTS KNEW THE FOLLOWING DARK SECRET: ON THE VERY DAY - NOVEMBER 9, 1918 - THAT GERMANY BECAME A REPUBLIC, THE NON-REVOLUTIONARY NATURE OF PRESIDENT EBERT'S GOVERNMENT WAS CONFIRMED WHEN HIS PHONE RANG IN HIS OFFICE IN THE CHANCELLERY. IT WAS ALREADY FAIRLY LATE IN THE EVENING. **EBERT** PICKED UP THE RECEIVER. ON THE OTHER END OF THE LINE WAS **GENERAL WILHELM GROENER,** WHO'D REPLACED ERICH LUDENDORFF AS QUARTER-MASTER GENERAL (THE OFFICER IN CHARGE OF SUPPLIES FOR THE WHOLE ARMY).

If the army offers assistance against forces of the left that might threaten your government, will you accept it?
Yes
General Groener
President Ebert

THE TWO MEN AGREED THAT THE GOVERNMENT WOULDN'T TRY TO REFORM THE ARMY IF THE ARMY SWORE TO PROTECT THE STATE.

THIS AGREEMENT IS KNOWN AS THE "**EBERT-GROENER PACT**". IT SYMBOLIZED THE ACCEPTANCE OF THE NEW GOVERNMENT BY THE MILITARY.

EBERT NEEDED SOMEONE FROM HIS PARTY TO DO THE DIRTY WORK AGAINST THE REVOLUTIONARIES...

Gustav Noske

GUSTAV NOSKE, THE MINISTER OF INTERIOR, VOLUNTEERED TO BE THE "BLOODHOUND OF THE REVOLUTION".

Noske's job was to hunt down, arrest, and if necessary, kill the revolutionaries.

NOSKE WORKED TOGETHER WITH GENERAL GROENER, WHO USED TROOPS FROM A BASE OUTSIDE BERLIN.

THE TROOPS WERE HELPED BY EXTREME RIGHT-WING NATIONALIST VOLUNTEERS - THE ***FREIKORPS,*** OR "FREE CORPS", AND THEY DROWNED THE COMMUNIST REBELLION IN **BLOOD.**

"Order reigns in Berlin!" You foolish lackeys! Your "order" is built on sand. Tomorrow the revolution will rise up again, clashing its weapons, and to your horror will proclaim, trumpets blazing: *I was, I am, I shall be!*

Rosa Luxemburg

Their revolution defeated, Rosa Luxemburg and Karl Liebknecht hid in a friend's apartment.

NOSKE GAVE THE ORDER TO FIND THE TWO COMMUNIST LEADERS.

THEY WERE SOON DISCOVERED BY A *FREIKORPS* UNIT UNDER THE COMMAND OF A **CAPTAIN WALDEMAR PABST.**

Captain Waldemar Pabst

I AM FROM TODAY

KARL AND ROSA WERE HAULED OFF TO HOTEL EDEN, TEMPORARY HEADQUARTERS FOR CAPTAIN PABST'S UNIT.

EDEN HOTEL

We'll go through the motions of interrogating these two Communists, then pretend to be taking them to Moabit Prison.
Eden Hotel
ROSA

That woman we just brought in is Rosa Luxemburg, a Communist devil. You'll shoot her when she comes back out.
Sir, there are people here. I might hit someone by accident.

The order will be carried out, Sir.
Then kill her with the butt of your rifle.

Eden Hotel
ROSA
Eden Hotel
ROSA
HOTEL
5783
BANG
BANG
5783

THEN THEY THREW HER BODY INTO ONE OF BERLIN'S CANALS...

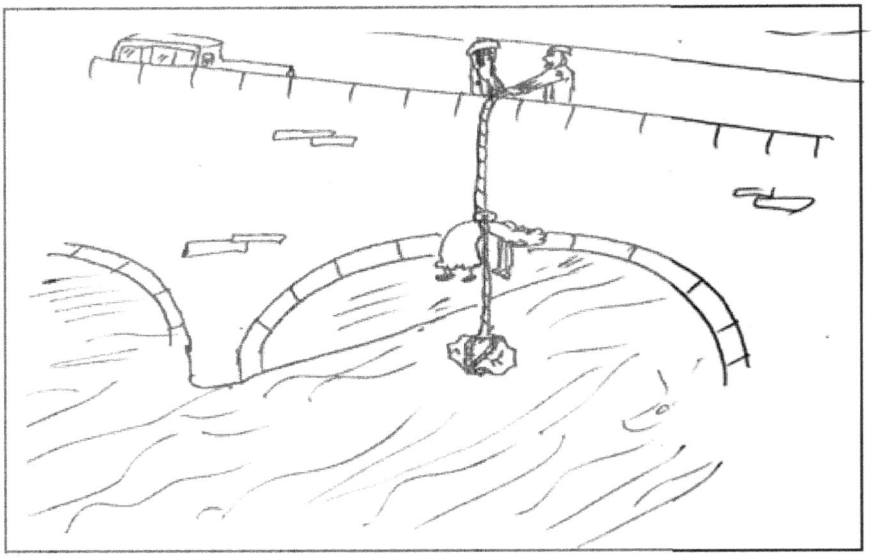

CAPTAIN PABST'S *FREIKORPS* MEN KILLED KARL LIEBKNECHT A LITTLE LATER ON.

CAPTAIN PABST WAS NEVER PUNISHED. HE LIVED TO THE RIPE OLD AGE OF 89, DYING OF NATURAL CAUSES IN THE CITY OF DÜSSELDORF IN 1970.

To stay in power, Ebert's SPD government walked over the corpses of Communists!

EVEN THOUGH THE *FREIKORPS* WAS A MILITARY UNIT, IT WASN'T PART OF THE OFFICIAL ARMY SO THOSE RESPONSIBLE FOR THE MURDER OF ROSA LUXEMBURG AND KARL LIEBKNECHT WEREN'T TRIED BEFORE A COURT MARTIAL (A COURT FOR SOLDIERS, WHICH IS MUCH STRICTER THAN A COURT FOR CIVILIANS).

Who said what goes around necessarily comes around?

THE SENTENCES HANDED DOWN TO THE FEW PEOPLE WHO WERE PUT ON TRIAL WERE VERY MUCH LIGHTER THAN THE CRIMES WARRANTED.

EBERT'S SOCIAL DEMOCRATIC GOVERNMENT WAS EXTREMELY UNPOPULAR AMONG THE REVOLUTIONARIES, WHO NEVER FORGOT THAT IT HAD USED THE EXTREME RIGHT-WING *FREIKORPS* TO CRUSH THEIR ATTEMPTED REVOLUTION.

Freikorps men display a captured Spartacist.

THE *FREIKORPS* WERE AN ARMY OUTSIDE THE CONTROL OF THE GOVERNMENT, BUT ONE WHICH HAD CLOSE ALLIES IN THE REGULAR ARMY. MOST OF ITS MEMBERS WERE SOLDIERS DISHARGED AT THE END OF THE WAR.

WHAT REALLY WORRIED EBERT'S GOVERNMENT WAS THAT ITS HAVING WORKED TOGETHER WITH THE *FREIKORPS* AND THE ARMY TO CRUSH THE COMMUNISTS DIDN'T REMOVE THE THREAT TO IT FROM THE RIGHT.
These are dangerous games to play.
Eberts' Social Democratic government cut a deal with us. And when you deal with us, you're indebted *forever!*

No civilian government will control us!

ONE OF THE RIGHT-WING FREE CORPS UNITS WAS THE **MARINEBRIGADE ERHARDT**, WHICH HAD THE **SWASTIKA** AS ITS RECOGNITION SYMBOL (AS ON THE SOLDER BELOW; HITLER AND HIS **NAZI PARTY** WOULD ADOPT IT AS THEIR OWN IN 1920).

THE SWASTIKA IS FOUND IN MANY CULTURES, INCLUDING THE INDIAN, CHINESE, JAPANESE AND SOUTHERN EUROPEAN. *SWASTIKA* IN SANSKRIT MEANS "TO BE GOOD", AND STANDS FOR LIFE, POWER, SUN, STRENGTH AND GOOD LUCK.

GERMAN NATIONALISTS ADOPTED IT IN THE 19TH CENTURY BECAUSE IT WAS ASSOCIATED WITH THE ANCIENT ARIAN RACE OF NORTHERN EUROPE OR CENTRAL ASIA, FROM WHOM MOST OF THE EUROPEAN RACES ARE DESCENDED.

TO HITLER AND THE NAZIS, THE SWASTIKA SYMBOLIZED THE VICTORY OF THE ARYAN RACE, OF THE WHITE MAN.

THE PROBLEM FOR EBERT'S GOVERNMENT WAS THAT THE RIGHT-WING "MAFIOSI" WHO HELPED THEM PUT DOWN THE COMMUNISTS HATED HIM AND HIS SOCIAL DEMOCRATS ALMOST AS MUCH AS THEY HATED THE REDS.

The SPD leaders knew this and worried about it.

IN THE MEANTIME, ELECTIONS WERE HELD ON JANUARY 19, 1919. THESE WERE THE FIRST IN GERMANY IN WHICH WOMEN VOTED. ALSO, THE VOTING AGE WAS LOWERED FOR EVERYONE FROM 25 TO 20.

These were the first truly free and fair all-German elections.

THE 1919 ELECTIONS WERE THE FIRST TO BE HELD AFTER THE SCRAPPING OF THE OLD VOTING SYSTEM WHICH HEAVILY OVERREPRESENTED RURAL AREAS, AREAS WHERE THE COUNTRY'S TRADITIONAL ELITE, THE LANDOWNING *JUNKER* ARISTOCRATS, LIVED. THIS HAD GIVEN AN UNFAIR ADVANTAGE TO THE *JUNKERS*.

30 MILLION GERMAN MEN AND WOMEN OVER THE AGE OF TWENTY ELECTED 423 DEPUTIES TO REPRESENT THEM IN THE NATIONAL ASSEMBLY WHICH HAD THE TASK OF GIVING GERMANY A NEW CONSTITUTION AND MAKING PEACE WITH THE ALLIES.

Die Verfassung

The very first elections revealed a major problem for the Social Democrats: right-wirg parties did relatively well.

BUT THE GERMAN REPUBLIC'S FIRST ELECTIONS WERE A BIT OF A DISAPPOINTMENT FOR THE SOCIAL DEMOCRATS. ALTHOUGH THE S.P.D CAME IN FIRST WITH OVER 11.500,000 VOTES OR 37 PERCENT OF THE TOTAL, THEY DIDN'T HAVE A WORKING MAJORITY IN PARLIAMENT. THIS MEANT THAT THEY NEEDED THE SUPPORT OF THE CATHOLIC CENTER PARTY, WHICH CAME IN SECOND WITH 5,900,000 OR 19 PERCENT.

It hadn't been very long since Germany's defeat in the war, and the right-wing was making a come-back!

THE MONARCHIST *DEUTSCH NATIONALE* PARTY GOT 2,600,000 VOTES OR 8.6 PERCENT OF THE TOTAL, AND THE NATIONAL PEOPLE'S PARTY (D.N.V.P), REPRESENTING BIG INDUSTRIALISTS (FACTORY OWNERS) WHO WANTED TO RETURN TO THE "GOOD OLD DAYS" OF *KAISER* WILHELM'S GERMANY (WHICH IS KNOWN AS WILHELMINE GERMANY), MANAGED TO GET 1,300,000 VOTES.

THE LITTLE TOWN OF WEIMAR WAS CHOSEN FOR THE NATIONAL ASSEMBLY.

Ebert wanted to remind the victors of WWI of Weimar Classicism, which included the likes of Goethe, Schiller, and the philosopher Herder.
Maybe so, but the main reason was purely military.
GERMAN

BERLIN WAS TOO DANGEROUS AT THE TIME, WITH ALL KINDS OF ARMED MEN RUNNING AROUND, AND THE TOWN OF WEIMAR WAS THOUGHT TO BE THE RIGHT SIZE TO BE EASILY DEFENDED BY *FREIKORPS* TROOPS.

What?! The National Assembly was defended by the proto-fascist *Freikorps*?!
Yup - the same men who'd brutally just put down the Spartacists and killed Rosa Luxemburg and Karl Liebknecht.

ON FEBRUARY 11, 1919, THE ASSEMBLY ELECTED FRIEDRICH EBERT PRESIDENT OF THE FIRST OFFICIAL GOVERNMENT OF POST WAR GERMANY, THE **WEIMAR REPUBLIC.**

PHILIPP SCHEIDEMANN WAS ELECTED CHANCELLOR.

THE FIRST SERIOUS CHALLENGE TO THE WEIMAR REPUBLIC CAME FROM MUNICH, THE CAPITAL OF BAVARIA. WE'VE SEEN THAT BACK ON NOVEMBER 8, 1918, EXACTLY ONE DAY BEFORE THE *KAISER* ABDICATED, A GROUP OF COMMUNISTS AND ANARCHISTS LED BY ACTOR AND MEMBER OF THE INDEPENDENT SOCIALIST PARTY (U.S.P.D), KURT EISNER, TOOK OVER THE BAVARIAN GOVERNMENT, OVERTHREW THE MONARCHY, AND DECLARED THE BIRTH OF A "FREE BAVARIAN REPUBLIC".

Germany's ruling elites are responsible for WWI!
Shut up, you communist swine!

Right-winger

Kurt Eisner

INFURIATED BY HIS CONSTANT CRITICISM, THE RIGHT-WING ASSASSINATED KURT EISNER IN APRIL OF 1919.

THIS LED EISNER'S COMMUNISTS TO RAMP UP THEIR REPUBLIC, WHICH THEY NOW CALLED A **"BAVARIAN SOVIET REPUBLIC"**.

THEY BEGAN TO TAKE OVER ESTATES FROM THE RICH AND GIVE THEM TO THE POOR, AND DO THINGS IN THIS REVOLUTIONARY SPIRIT.

IN RESPONSE, 30,000 *FREIKORPS* MEN CAME TO MUNICH IN MAY 1919 AND ATTACKED THE COMMUNISTS.

IN BITTER STREET-FIGHTING, THE *FREIKORPS* KILLED 1,000 AND EXECUTED ANOTHER 700 THEY'D TAKEN PRISONER....

.....AND THAT ENDED THE SHORT-LIVED BAVARIAN SOVIET REPUBLIC.

Bavaria's a great place for us right-wingers!

AFTER THEIR VICTORY, MANY OF THE EXTREMIST RIGHT-WINGERS DECIDED TO REMAIN IN BAVARIA.

Plus the beer and *wienerschnitsels* are excellent!

THIS WAS A TIME WHEN FAR-RIGHT MOVEMENTS AND ORGANIZATIONS IN BAVARIA FLOURISHED, INCLUDING THE ORGANIZATION CONSUL, THE GERMAN WORKERS' PARTY (D.A.P. WHICH WE'LL SEE BECAME THE NAZI PARTY), AND ALSO GROUPS OF EXILED RUSSIAN MONARCHISTS WHO WANTED TO OVERTHROW LENIN'S COMMUNISTS.

SPORADIC FIGHTING CONTINUED TO FLARE UP AROUND THE COUNTRY BETWEEN THE LEFT AND THE RIGHT. THIS WAS A MINI CIVIL WAR: IN EASTERN GERMAN PROVINCES, FORCES LOYAL TO GERMANY'S FALLEN MONARCHY FOUGHT THE REPUBLIC, WHILE MILITIAS OF POLISH NATIONALISTS FOUGHT FOR INDEPENDENCE, ESPECIALLY IN POSEN. THERE WERE ALSO THREE UPRISINGS IN UPPER SILESIA AS LOCAL POLES TRIED (BUT FAILED) TO SEPARATE OUT FROM GERMANY AND JOIN POLAND.

IN THE MEANTIME, BACK IN THE LITTLE TOWN OF WEIMAR, A CONSTITUTION WAS FINALLY SIGNED IN JULY 1919; IT MADE THE PARLIAMENT THE MAIN AUTHORITY IN GERMANY.

Grrrrr...

Yes!

That was a major break from Bismarck's constitution!

THE OLD JUNKER-CONTROLLED *REICHSRAT*, OR UPPER HOUSE OF PARLIAMENT, CONTINUED TO REPRESENT THE DIFFERENT GERMAN STATES, BUT NOW IT WAS SUBORDINATE TO THE *REICHSTAG*, OR LOWER HOUSE OF PARLIAMENT.

ACCORDING TO THE NEW LAW OF THE LAND, PARLIAMENT WAS TO BE ELECTED EVERY 4 YEARS BY MEN AND WOMEN OVER 21.
German women got the right to vote much earlier than women in most other countries!
So? We men got the vote much earlier than other countries, too, and what was the result?
Women are by nature more progressive.
You sure about that?
THIS WAS ALL FINE AND WELL, BUT THERE WAS SOMETHING ABOUT THE NEW CONSTITUTION THAT WAS DISTURBINGLY SIMILAR TO THE OLD *REICH* UNDER BISMARCK. THE STRENGTHS IT GAVE TO THE PRESIDENT WERE ABOUT AS GREAT AS THE *KAISER* HAD ENJOYED.
For a people as addicted to the worship of authority as the Germans, the President's powers were dangerously vast!

THE PRESIDENT OF THE WEIMAR REPUBLIC WAS ELECTED EVERY SEVEN YEARS.

THAT'S A PRETTY LONG TIME, RIGHT?

HE WAS ALSO COMMANDER-IN-CHIEF OF THE ARMED FORCES AND HAD THE RIGHT TO APPOINT AND DISMISS NOT ONLY OFFICERS, BUT THE CHANCELLOR AND HIS MINISTERS, TOO.

MOST IMPORTANT AND DANGEROUS OF ALL WAS THE FACT THAT UNDER **ARTICLE 48** OF THE NEW CONSTITUTION THE **PRESIDENT** COULD SUSPEND THE CIVIL RIGHTS OF THE CITIZENS IN AN EMERGENCY. IN OTHER WORDS, HE HAD THE RIGHT TO ACT LIKE A DICTATOR AND DO THINGS WITHOUT PARLIAMENT'S APPROVAL.

It was never defined what exactly an "emergency" was.

LET'S TAKE STOCK OF THE **TIME BOMBS** PLACED EARLY ON UNDER THE FRAGILE WEIMAR REPUBLIC.

WEIMAR DEMOCRACY

THESE INCLUDED:

* THE SECRET ALLIANCE BETWEEN EBERT AND GROENER
* THE RESULTING RELIANCE BY THE GOVERNMENT ON THE SUPPORT OF THE ANTI-DEMOCRATIC *FREIKORPS*
* THE SUICIDAL DIVISION AMONG THE SOCIALIST FOUNDERS OF THE REPUBLIC
* THE ANTI-DEMOCRATIC RIGHTS OF THE PRESIDENT
* THE BELIEF OF THE GERMAN PEOPLE THAT THEIR COUNTRY WAS THE INNOCENT VICTIM OF A WAR OF AGGRESSION BY ENEMIES WHO WERE JEALOUS OF THE *REICH'S* GROWING POWER AND PROSPERITY.

This propaganda was so intense that if someone openly doubted Germany's innocence, he or she was treated as a traitor and locked up in prison!
LONG BEFORE ADOLF HITLER, ORDINARY GERMANS FELT MORALLY JUSTIFIED AS PATRIOTS TO GO AGAINST THE "TRAITOR REPUBLIC". THEY DID THIS BY EVADING TAXATION OR SABOTAGING IT IN OTHER WAYS.
Ironically, Ebert's government undermined itself by supporting the propaganda campaign that denied Imperial Germany's guilt in WWI!
SO DESPITE THE POSITIVE CHANGES, PEOPLE'S POLITICAL ATTITUDES HADN'T CHANGED IN GERMANY AFTER THE END OF THE OLD EMPIRE. IN THE LONG RUN, THIS DOOMED THE WEIMAR REPUBLIC TO FAILURE.

THE TREATY OF VERSAILLES

THE GERMANS HAD EXPECTED THAT THE ALLIES WOULD BE IMPRESSED BY THE ABDICATION OF THE *KAISER*, AND BY THEIR SOCIAL DEMOCRATIC GOVERNMENT. THEY TRULY BELIEVED THE ALLIES WOULD GRANT THEM A PEACE TREATY BASED UPON AMERICAN PRESIDENT WILSON'S LIBERAL 14 POINTS, HIS PLAN FOR A NEW WORLD BASED ON DEMOCRACY, PEACE AND THE MUTUAL RESPECT OF NATIONS.

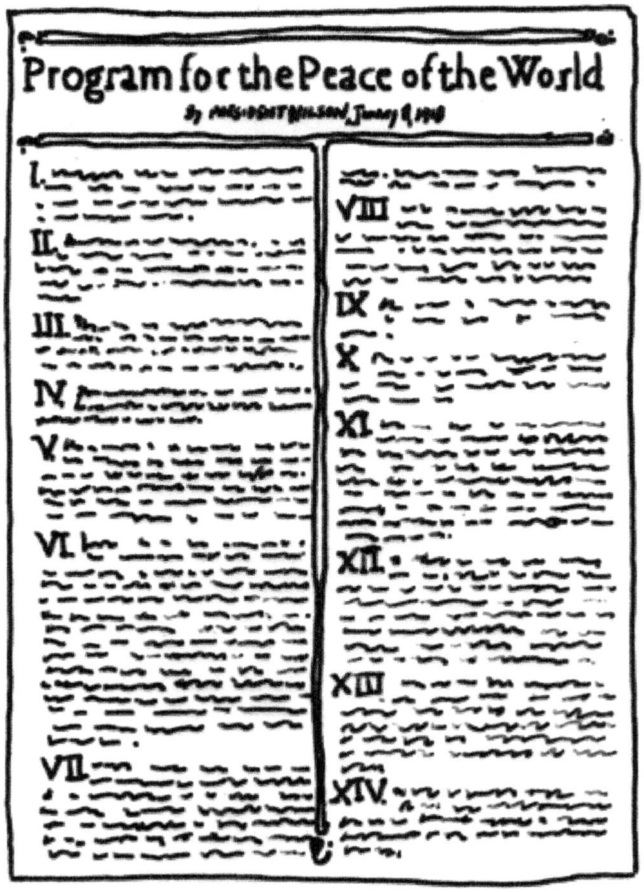
Program for the Peace of the World

When, in October 1918, Generals Hindenburg and Ludendorff had asked me, Prince Max Von Baden, to negotiate an armistice for our defeated army, all they really wanted was a cease-fire that would give them time to recover and regroup for a second bid for world-power.

Ebert's secret alliance with General Groener made that second bid inevitable.
GERMAN

THE GERMANS WERE CONVINCED THAT THE PEACE TREATY WOULD SHOW NONE OF THE HARSHNESS THEY THEMSELVES HAD DISPLAYED IN THE TREATY THEY'D IMPOSED ON THE RUSSIANS AT BREST-LITOVSK IN MARCH OF 1918. THE TREATY OF BREST-LITOVSK HAD FORCED THE RUSSIANS TO SURRENDER NEARLY HALF OF THEIR EUROPEAN TERRITORY, AS WELL AS FINLAND, THE BALTIC PROVINCES, BELORUSSIA, THE UKRAINE, POLAND, AND PARTS OF THE CAUCASUS.

And don't forget the harsh September 1914 peace aims of "moderate" Chancellor Bethmann-Hollweg that called for grabbing land from France and Belgium and forcing crippling reparations on the Entente!

AT VERSAILLES, THE LEADERS OF THE MAIN ALLIED POWERS - FRANCE, BRITAIN, THE UNITED STATES OF AMERICA AND ITALY - TALKED FOR SIX MONTHS, FROM JANUARY TO JUNE, 1919.

Orlando (Italy)
Lloyd George (U.K.)
Cllemenceau (France)
Wilson (U.S.A.)

AT VERSAILLES THE GERMANS WERE MADE TO FEEL LIKE *PERSONA NON GRATA* - TOTALLY UNDESIRABLE.

This German political cartoon shows Germany as an innocent victim of the victors, who want to guillotine it.

It's ironic the French, who were treated so well in 1815 after the fall of Napoleon, hosted such a bully show against the Germans.
Do you know what it feels like to be snubbed by the French?
GERNAN

THIS CONTRASTED SHARPLY TO THE WAY DEFEATED NAPOLEONIC FRANCE HAD BEEN TREATED BACK IN 1815 AT THE CONGRESS OF VIENNA, WHEN IT WAS INVITED TO PARTICIPATE IN THE DISCUSSIONS. THE FRENCH DELEGATE, CHARLES TALLEYRAND, HAD MANAGED TO GET A DEAL THAT WASN'T DISASTROUS FOR FRANCE.

Plus I danced and flirted with the ladies!

Charles Maurice de Talleyrand

THE ALLIED LEADERS AT VERSAILLES WERE UNDER GREAT PRESSURE FROM THEIR ANGRY PEOPLE BACK HOME TO PUNISH GERMANY.

British Prime Minister
David Lloyd George

HANG THE KAISER!
SQUEEZE THE GERMAN LEMON UNTIL THE PIPS SQUEAK!!

British patriots

FRANCE, ABOVE ALL ELSE, WANTED SECURITY FOR THE FUTURE. THERE WAS NO LIMIT TO HOW MUCH IT WOULD PRESSURE GERMANY.

The losses we French suffered must *never* be repeated!

...BRITAIN WAS MORE FLEXIBLE.

THE BRITISH GOVERNMENT DIDN'T WANT GERMANY TO BE TOO WEAK. TO THE EAST WAS NOW COMMUNIST RUSSIA, AND A WEAK GERMANY WASN'T GOOD FOR THE BALANCE OF POWER IN EUROPE OR FOR INTERNATIONAL TRADE AND BUSINESS.

THE SCUTTLING BY THE GERMANS OF THEIR FLEET AT SCAPA FLOW IN SCOTLAND ON JUNE 31, 1919, MADE THE BRITISH FEEL SAFER ABOUT THE FUTURE.

We don't want Germany to become a victim of the Soviet regime in Russia.
BRITON
What does he mean?
That if pressed too hard, Germany might turn communist! Can you imagine having two major communist countries in Europe, Russia *and* Germany?!

AMERICAN **PRESIDENT WILSON** WAS A DEEPLY RELIGIOUS PRESBYTERIAN WHO REGULARLY READ HIS BIBLE.

U.S. President Woodrow Wilson

He brought a religious style of idealism to American diplomacy. God bless him!

WILSON WAS THE MAIN FORCE AT VERSAILLES. HE WANTED A **"PEACE WITHOUT VICTORY"** AND NO SELFISHNESS FROM ANYONE.

America's naïve prophet of peace wants to replace the corrupt European diplomacy with a system based on justifiable national claims.

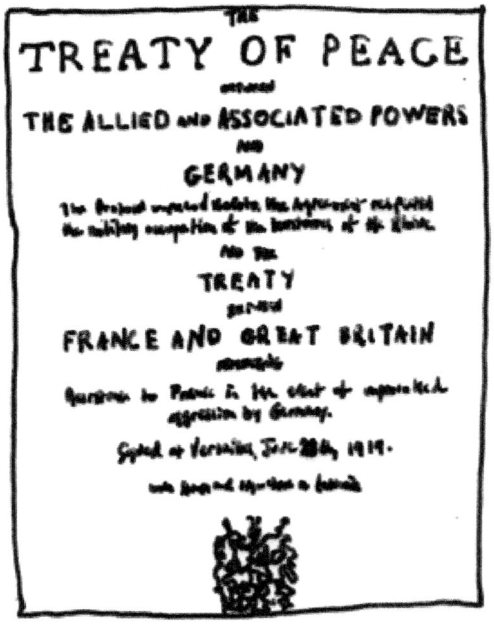
TREATY OF PEACE
THE ALLIED AND ASSOCIATED POWERS
GERMANY
TREATY
FRANCE AND GREAT BRITAIN

FINALLY, ON MAY 7, 1919, THE GERMANS WERE CALLED TO VERSAILLES AND HANDED THE ALLIED PEACE TERMS.

THEY WERE...**STUNNED!**

The unbelievable has happened. Our enemies have presented us with a treaty which surpasses the worst fears of our pessimists.
The terms of the Treaty are totally unbearable!

Typical German politician

Friecrich Ebert

ALL OVER GERMANY, MASS PROTESTS WERE HELD.

ARTICLE 231 OF THE TREATY OF VERSAILLES BLAMED THE GERMANS FOR EVERYTHING.

Article 231 was the so-called "**War Guilt Clause**".
Look it up, man!

What's a clause, dude?

ALTHOUGH THE TREATY CALLED FOR THE EVENTUAL DISARMAMENT OF ALL COUNTRIES, **GERMANY** WAS **TO BE DISARMED IMMEDIATELY.**

That's a double standard!
GERMAN

NATURALLY AND QUITE JUSTIFIABLY, THE GERMANS THOUGHT THIS WAS TOTALLY AND COMPLETELY **UNFAIR.**

Shut up! *You* started the war!

THE GERMAN ARMY WAS TO HAVE ONLY 96,000 MEN AND 4,000 OFFICERS, THE MEN TO SERVE 12 YEARS, THE OFFICERS 24.
Smart move! That way they won't be able to build up experienced reserves.
THIS LIMIT ON SERVICE IN THE *REICHSWEHR* WAS A TERRIBLE BLOW TO THE GERMANS. THE PRESTIGE OF THE ARMY HAD BEEN MUCH GREATER IN GERMANY THAN IN ANY OTHER COUNTRY. AS WE SAW IN BOOK ONE, THE LIBERAL CIVILIAN POLITICIANS HAD FAILED TO UNITE THE COUNTRY IN THE REVOLUTION OF 1848, AND THE UNION HAD ONLY BEEN ACHIEVED BY FORCE OF PRUSSIAN ARMS IN 1871. SO IT WAS THE ARMY ELITE AND NOT CIVILIAN POLITICIANS WHO WERE SEEN AS THE BASIS AND FOUNDATION OF THE NATION.
The Treaty of Versailles prevents most of us Germans from taking part in an institution that we deeply admire and respect!
GERMANY WAS ALSO FORBIDDEN FROM HAVING OFFENSIVE WEAPONS: TANKS, HEAVY ARTILLERY, AIRCRAFT, SUBMARINES AND LARGE WARSHIPS.
And we're only allowed to have a tiny navy whose largest ship can't exceed 10,000 tons.

GERMANY'S BORDERS WERE CHANGED TO SATISFY THE DEMANDS OF NEIGHBORING NATIONALITIES.

IN THE WEST, ALSACE-LORRAINE WENT BACK TO FRANCE, AND THE SMALL REGIONS OF EUPEN AND MALMEDY TO BELGIUM. IN THE NORTH, NORTH SCHLESWIG WAS RETURNED TO THE DANES, AND LARGE AREAS IN THE EAST WERE GIVEN TO POLAND.

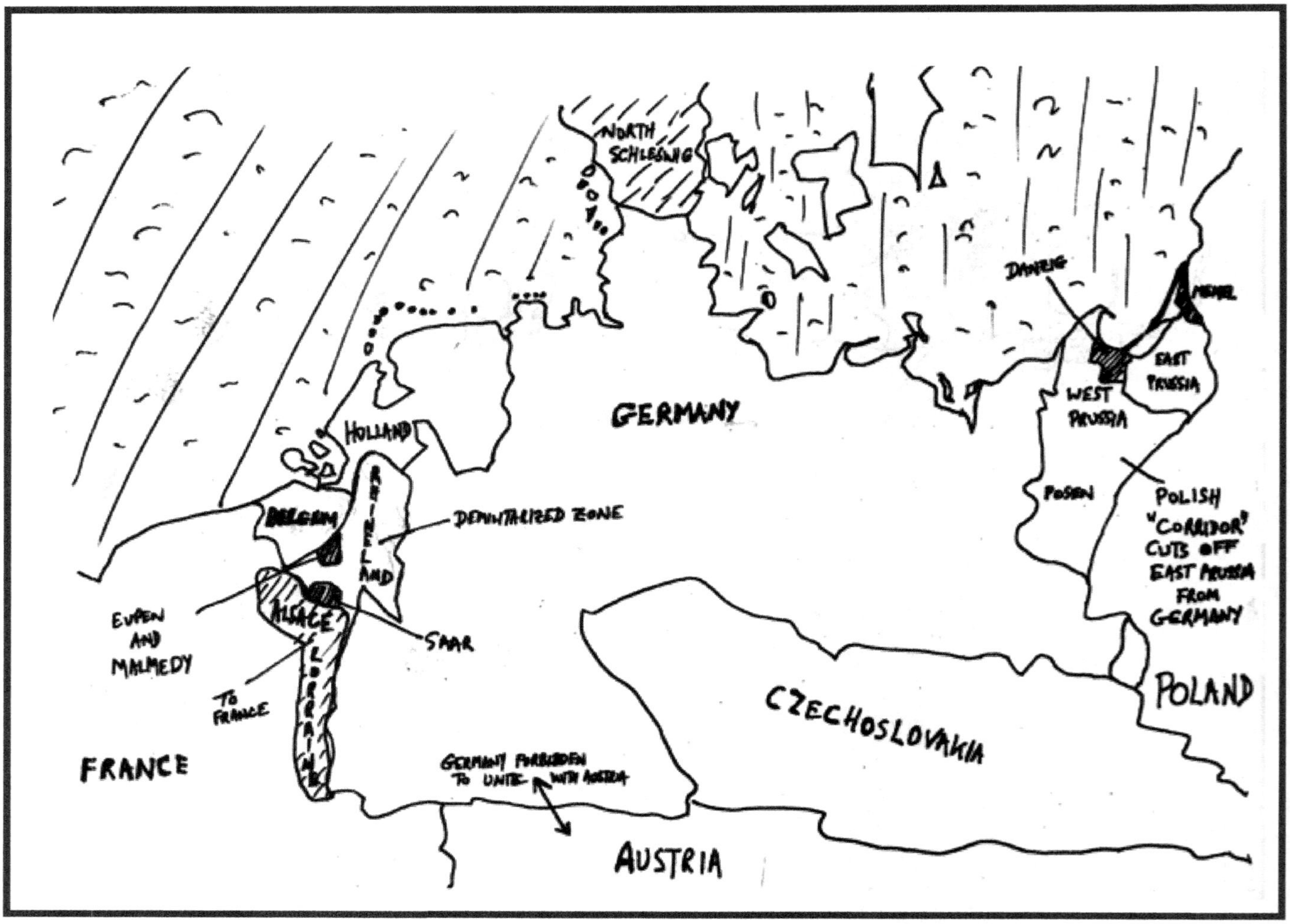

THE TREATY OF VERSAILLES ALSO SAID THAT THE RHINELAND WAS TO BE **OCCUPIED** BY ALLIED TROOPS FOR UP TO FIFTEEN YEARS.

TERRIFIED OF GERMANY EVEN IN DEFEAT, THE FRENCH HAD WANTED MORE FROM THE TREATY OF VERSAILLES. THEY WOULD'VE LOVED TO MOVE THEIR BORDER TO THE RHINE RIVER, AND MAKE THE RHINELAND FRENCH, OR AT LEAST CREATE AN INDEPENDENT NEUTRAL STATE THERE. BUT THE BRITISH AND THE AMERICANS REFUSED TO LET THEM DO SO.

TO THE GREAT INDIGNATION OF THE GERMANS, SOME OF THE FRENCH TROOPS IN THE RHINELAND WERE SENEGALESE. THESE MEN WERE DENOUNCED IN THE GERMAN PRESS AS THE "BLACK SHAME". (SEE THE DOUBLE RACISM OF THE GERMAN POSTER ON THE LEFT, WITH THE "EVIL JEW" IN THE BACKGROUND?)

The racist propaganda the Senegalese had to endure wasn't only German. Even the British press printed stories of the "Black Horror on the Rhine", making accusations that were based on hearsay and racial prejudice.

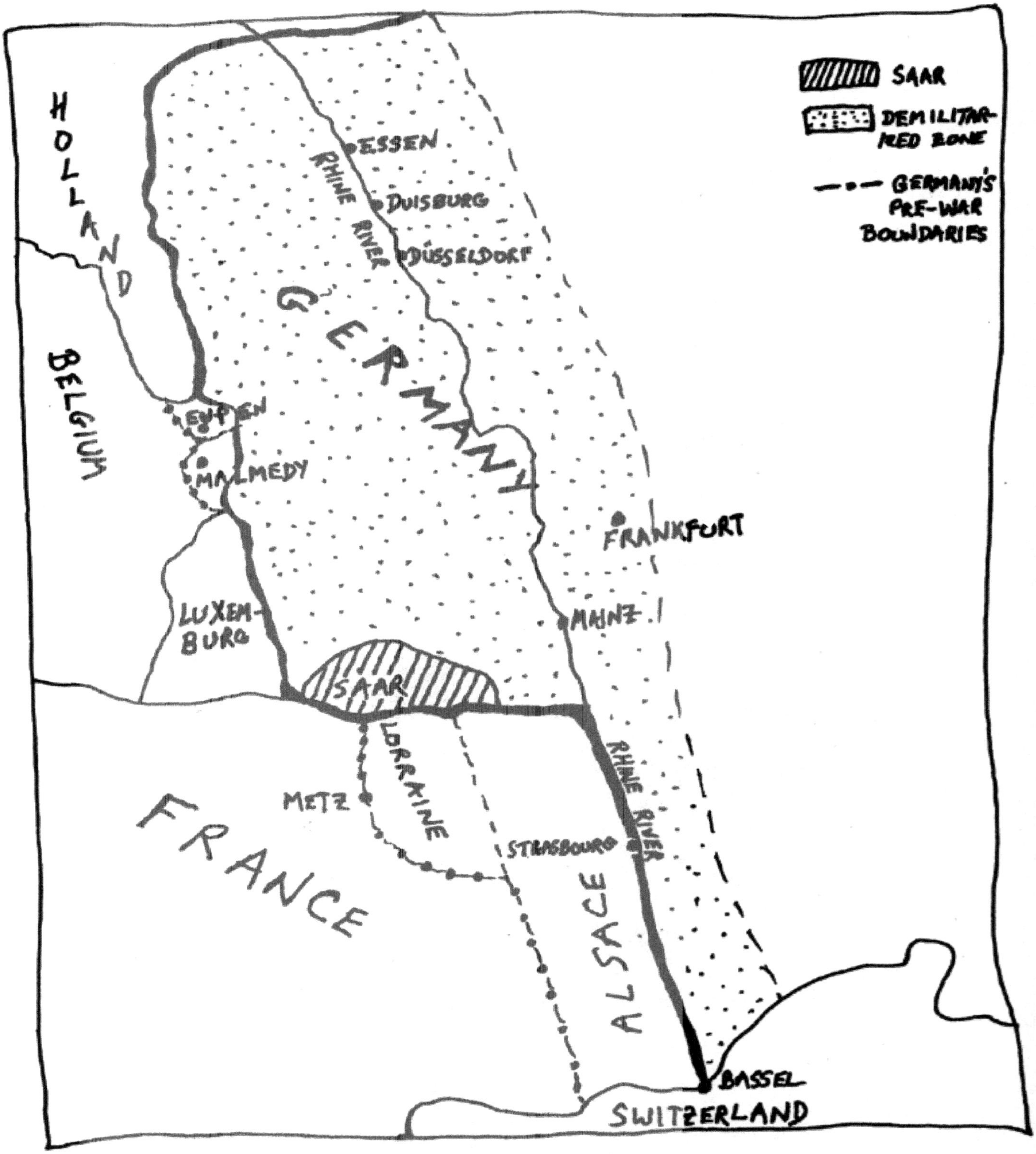

A STRIP FIFTY KILOMETERS WIDE ON THE EAST BANK OF THE RHINE WAS **DEMILITARIZED.** THIS MEANT THAT ALL GERMAN TROOPS WERE PERMANENTLY **BANNED FROM IT.**

So they never invade us again!
THE SAAR, A SMALL GERMAN TERRITORY ON THE BORDER WITH FRANCE, WAS TO BE ADMINISTERED INTERNATIONALLY BY THE **LEAGUE OF NATIONS** FOR 15 YEARS.
League of Nations?
US President Woodrow Wilson's idea - the first permanent organization set up after WWI to solve problems between countries via diplomacy, and not war. The League was the "mother" of today's UN.
THE ALLIES AT VERSAILLES DECIDED THAT IN 1935 A REFERENDUM WOULD BE HELD FOR THE LOCAL POPULATION IN THE SAAR TO DECIDE WHETHER THEY WANTED TO BELONG TO FRANCE OR TO GERMANY...

MOST GERMANS WERE FURIOUS WITH HOW THE TREATY OF VERSAILLES TOOK LAND AWAY FROM THE *REICH.*

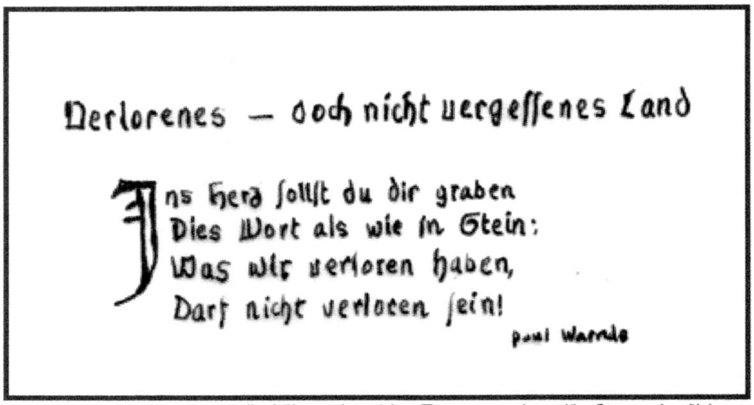

Verlorenes — doch nicht vergessenes Land

Ins Herz sollst du dir graben
Dies Wort als wie in Stein:
Was wir verloren haben,
Darf nicht verloren sein!

Paul Warncke

This contemporary poem is called "Lost but Not Forgotten Land". It reads: "You must carve in your heart these words, as in stone - what we have lost will be regained."

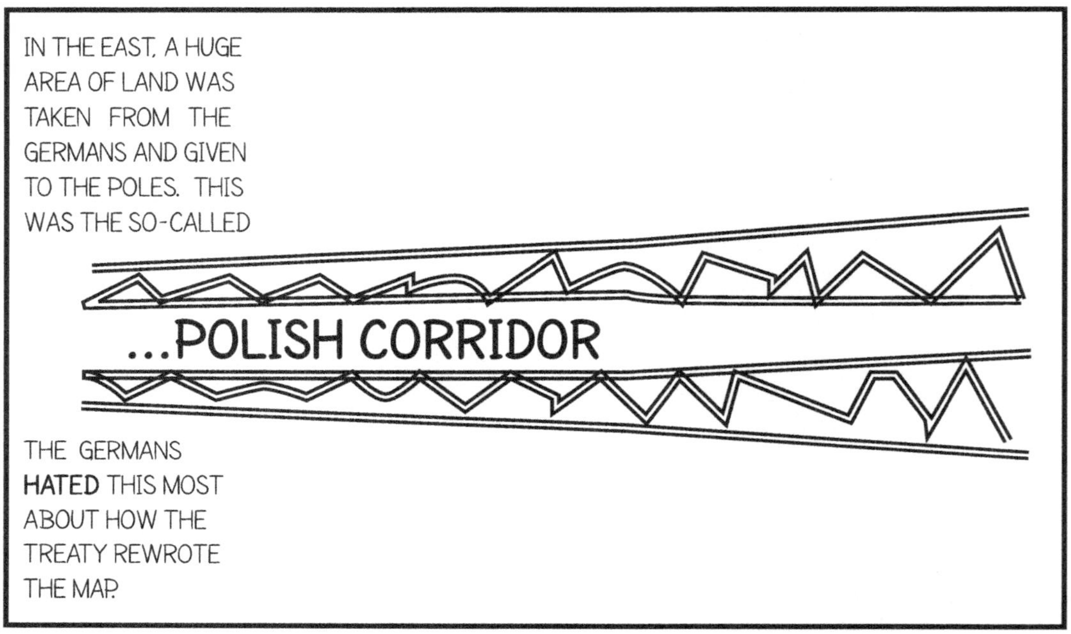
IN THE EAST, A HUGE AREA OF LAND WAS TAKEN FROM THE GERMANS AND GIVEN TO THE POLES. THIS WAS THE SO-CALLED
...POLISH CORRIDOR
THE GERMANS **HATED** THIS MOST ABOUT HOW THE TREATY REWROTE THE MAP.

We won the war against the Russians in the east! The Polish Corridor is totally **unfair!**
You Germans ***stole*** this land from us Poles in the partitions of Poland in the 18th century!
POLE

THE **POLISH CORRIDOR** GAVE THE NEW STATE OF POLAND ACCESS TO THE SEA.
New state?
POLAND WAS RECREATED AT VERSAILLES. IT HAD BEEN WIPED OFF THE MAP IN THE LATE 1700s, WHEN IT WAS REPEATEDLY PARTITIONED BY PRUSSIA, RUSSIA AND AUSTRIA...UNTIL NOTHING WAS LEFT OF THE COUNTRY.

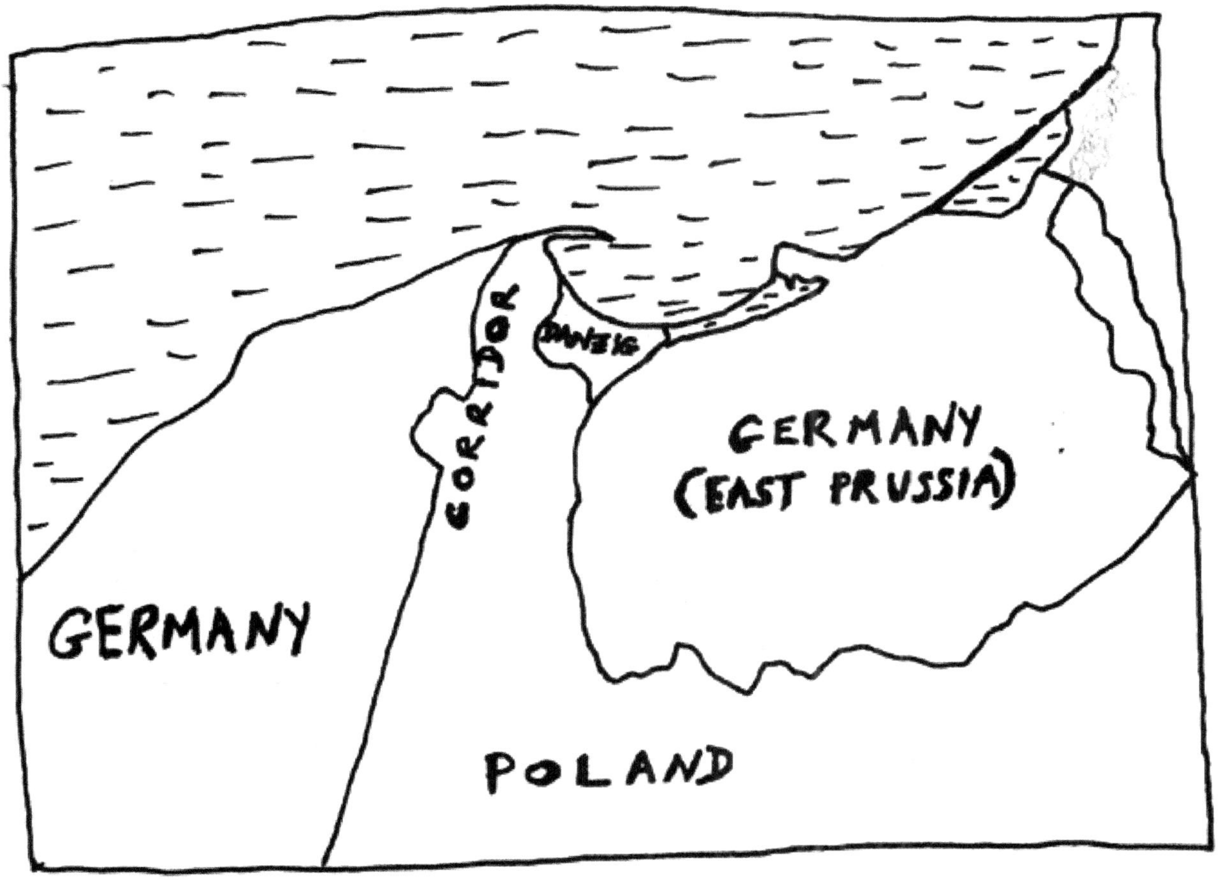
CORRIDOR
DANZIG
GERMANY (EAST PRUSSIA)
GERMANY
POLAND

AT THE END OF THE POLISH CORRIDOR, THE GERMAN CITY OF **DANZIG** NOW BECAME A "FREE CITY" UNDER INTERNATIONAL CONTROL, WITH POLAND ALLOWED TO USE ITS PORT.

Freie Stadt Danzig
REISE PASS

THE ALLIES CHARGED GERMANY FOR THE DAMAGE IT DID TO THEM IN THE WAR, YET THE BILL ALSO INCLUDED PENSIONS FOR WIDOWS AND MONEY FOR THE WAR WOUNDED. THESE ITEMS WERE ABOUT HALF THE TOTAL.

THE TREATY OF VERSAILLES INSISTED GERMANY PAY HUGE REPARATIONS.

Not me!
Who ever heard of charging for future pensions of war widows and crippled veterans?!
GERMAN

WHAT HAPPENED TO THE AUSTRO-HUNGARIAN EMPIRE ALSO CHANGED THE LOOK OF THE MAP TO THE EAST OF GERMANY. THE DISAPPEARANCE OF THE HABSBURG EMPIRE - A MAJOR PLAYER IN CENTRAL EUROPE FOR FIVE CENTURIES - LEFT THE GERMAN STATE OF AUSTRIA, BUT STRICTLY FORBADE IT TO UNITE WITH GERMANY.

A NUMBER OF NEW STATES APPEARED TO GERMANY'S EAST: YUGOSLAVIA, CZECHOSLOVAKIA AND POLAND.

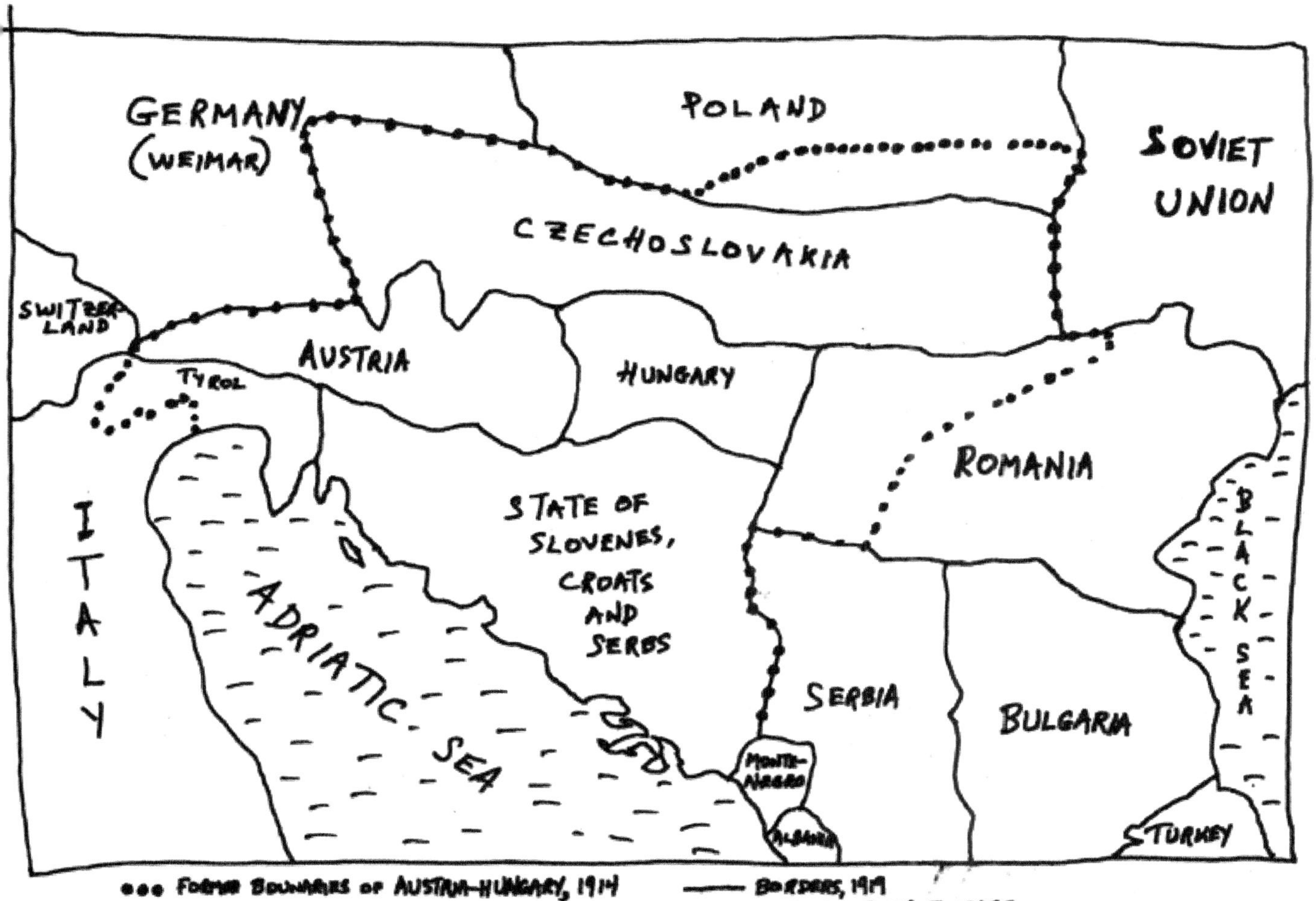

DISMEMBERMENT OF AUSTRO-HUNGARIAN EMPIRE

THESE NEW COUNTRIES WERE FORMED BY STRIPPING HUNGARY OF CROATIA, SLOVENIA, SLOVAKIA, AND RUTHENIA.

The decisions taken at Versailles weren't easy ones. They were much more difficult than those taken at the Congress of Vienna back in 1815.
THE TREATY OF VERSAILLES DIDN'T ALLOW GERMANY TO JOIN THE NEWLY-FORMED LEAGUE OF NATIONS, WITH ITS HEADQUARTERS IN THIS NICE BUILDING IN GENEVA, SWITZERLAND.
IN 1815, WHEN NAPOLEON BONAPARTE WAS DEFEATED, EUROPEAN LEADERS HAD TO REGULATE THE TERRITORIES OF DEFEATED NAPOLEONIC FRANCE. IN 1919, HOWEVER, THEY HAD TO DEAL WITH THOSE OF *FOUR* EMPIRES: GERMANY, TURKEY, AUSTRIA-HUNGARY, AND RUSSIA.

MOST GERMANS THOUGHT THE TREATY OF VERSAILLES TOO TOUGH AND UNFAIR. YET THEY THEMSELVES HAD SHOWN - WITH THE FRENCH IN 1871, AND THE RUSSIANS IN 1918 - NO GREAT MAGNANIMITY EITHER.

Lady *Germania* chained to a torture pole.

WHETHER OR NOT THE TREATY OF VERSAILLES WAS TOO HARD ON GERMANY IS A POINTLESS QUESTION TO TRY AND ANSWER. DEPENDING ON THEIR NATIONAL PREJUDICES, SOME PEOPLE LOOK AT THE INFORMATION AND SAY YES AND SOME SAY NO.

THE MAIN POINT IS THAT THE GERMANS DEFINITELY THOUGHT THE TREATY WAS VERY UNFAIR. WHETHER OR NOT THIS REFLECTED THEIR REAL ABILITY TO MEET ITS TERMS, IS ANOTHER QUESTION. WHAT MATTERS IS THAT THEY HONESTLY BELIEVED THIS WAS TRUE.

RATHER THAN SIGN, CHANCELLOR PHILIPP SCHEIDEMANN RESIGNED, ON JUNE 19, 1919.

May the hand wither that signs such a treaty!

Philipp Scheidemann

THE NEW GOVERNMENT WITH A MAN CALLED **GUSTAV BAUER** AS CHANCELLOR ALSO REFUSED TO SIGN THE HATED TREATY OF VERSAILLES.

We just won't sign!

Chancellor Gustav Bauer

IN THE END - AND WITH JUST NINETEEN MINUTES LEFT BEFORE THE DEADLINE - THE GERMANS DID SIGN THE TREATY OF VERSAILLES....BECAUSE THEY KNEW VERY WELL THAT OTHERWISE THE ALLIES WOULD IMMEDIATELY OCCUPY THE COUNTRY WITH THEIR FORCES.

In the foreground, the German delegation (Hermann Muller, standing, and Johannes Bell, sitting) signs the Treaty of Versailles, June 28, 1919.

BECAUSE THE GERMANS WERE SURE THEY WERE BEING VICTIMIZED, A NUMBER OF NON-GERMANS WERE EQUALLY CERTAIN THERE'D BE BIG PROBLEMS IN THE FUTURE.

This isn't peace. It's a truce for 20 years!

French General Ferdinand Foch

Wow, this guy's prediction was spot-on!

Mentalist Yuri Geller

Sore losers is what I call them!
I AM FROM TODA

THE GERMANS, WHO'D HAD THE HIGHEST STANDARD OF LIVING IN EUROPE BEFORE THE WAR, AND HAD NEVER LOST BATTLES SINCE 1871, WHEN THEIR EMPIRE WAS FOUNDED, SIMPLY REFUSED TO ACCEPT THE FACT OF DEFEAT.

WHAT DID EBERT'S GOVERNMENT DO?
IT FOLLOWED A POLICY OF OBSTRUCTION.
We're not going to make it easy for the Allies to get what they want from us.
When one signs under duress there's no question of insincerity. There's a big difference between signing and fulfilling an agreement.

Friedrich Ebert

Matthias Erzberger, who signed the Armistice for Germany in November 1918.

I prefer death to surrendering to the Allies!
He looks pretty comfortable in Holland.
PEACE
THE HIPPIE FROM TODAY
Kaiser Wilhelm II

DRAGGING ITS FEET, THE GERMAN GOVERNMENT DIDN'T DISBAND THE VARIOUS PARAMILITARY ORGANIZATIONS THAT HAD SPRUNG UP AFTER THE ARMISTICE IN 1918.

AS FOR THE REGULAR ARMY, THEY WOULD ONLY DISARM IT UNDER CONSTANT ALLIED SUPERVISION.

...FOR ALL THESE REASONS, THE MAIN PROBLEM THAT HAUNTED EUROPE FOR THE NEXT TWO DECADES WAS **GERMAN RESENTMENT**.

We'd hoped for fair treatment! Instead we were presented with a *diktat* that stripped our Reich of 25,000 square miles or 13% of the land, and 7 million people or 10% of our total population.
GERMAN
You started the war!
FRENCH

THE TREATY OF VERSAILLES HAD SHORTCOMINGS THAT WERE SO OBVIOUS THEY WERE EMBARRASSING. MOST TERRITORIAL CHANGES AFTER THE WAR WERE MADE BASED ON THE PRINCIPLE OF NATIONALITY. THIS MEANT THAT PEOPLE OF THE SAME NATIONALITY WERE SUPPOSED TO LIVE IN THE SAME COUNTRY....

Why are we northern Germans forbidden from uniting with all the German-speakers of Austria?!
...BUT THERE WERE **DOUBLE STANDARDS.**
We've been stripped of all our colonies while the victors have kept theirs - and even added colonies to their empires!

FACED WITH THESE REALITIES, MANY GERMANS NEEDED A JUSTIFICATION FOR WHY THEIR LIFE HAD SUDDENLY GONE FROM PRETTY GOOD TO VERY BAD.
Don't look at me! As a simple factory worker I can't say my life'd been excellent before the Great War.
MOST PEOPLE REACTED BY REFUSING TO ACKNOWLEDGE THEY'D BEEN BEATEN. THIS WAS EASIER TO SQUARE WITH THEIR REFUSAL TO COMPLY WITH THE DEMANDS OF THE TREATY OF VERSAILLES.
GERMAN FACTORY WORKER

We weren't defeated!

DER DOLCHSTOSS

SO THE MYTH OF THE **STAB-IN-THE-BACK**, THE ***DOLCHSTOSS LEGENDE***, WAS BORN.

MANY GERMANS TRULY BELIEVED THAT THE WEIMAR REPUBLIC WASN'T THE "CHILD" OF THE NEW CONSTITUTION, BUT RATHER THAT OF THE FOREIGN-IMPOSED TREATY OF VERSAILLES.

What a laugh! As if the German army had a snowball's chance in hell of winning if the war had continued!

Remember, the Constitution was signed in July, 1919, very shortly after Versailles!

DESPITE HER DEFEAT IN THE FIRST WORLD WAR, AND NOTWITHSTANDING THE STRICT WAY THE TREATY PUNISHED HER OR THE EMOTIONAL MANNER IN WHICH HER PEOPLE REACTED ANGRILY TO THE TREATY OF VERSAILLES, THE FACT WAS THAT GERMANY CONTINUED TO HAVE THE STRONGEST ECONOMY IN EUROPE.

This wouldn't be the case had the war been allowed to continue!

It *should've* been continued. If Germany's ruling elites had been crushed, then maybe there wouldn't have been a Second World War.

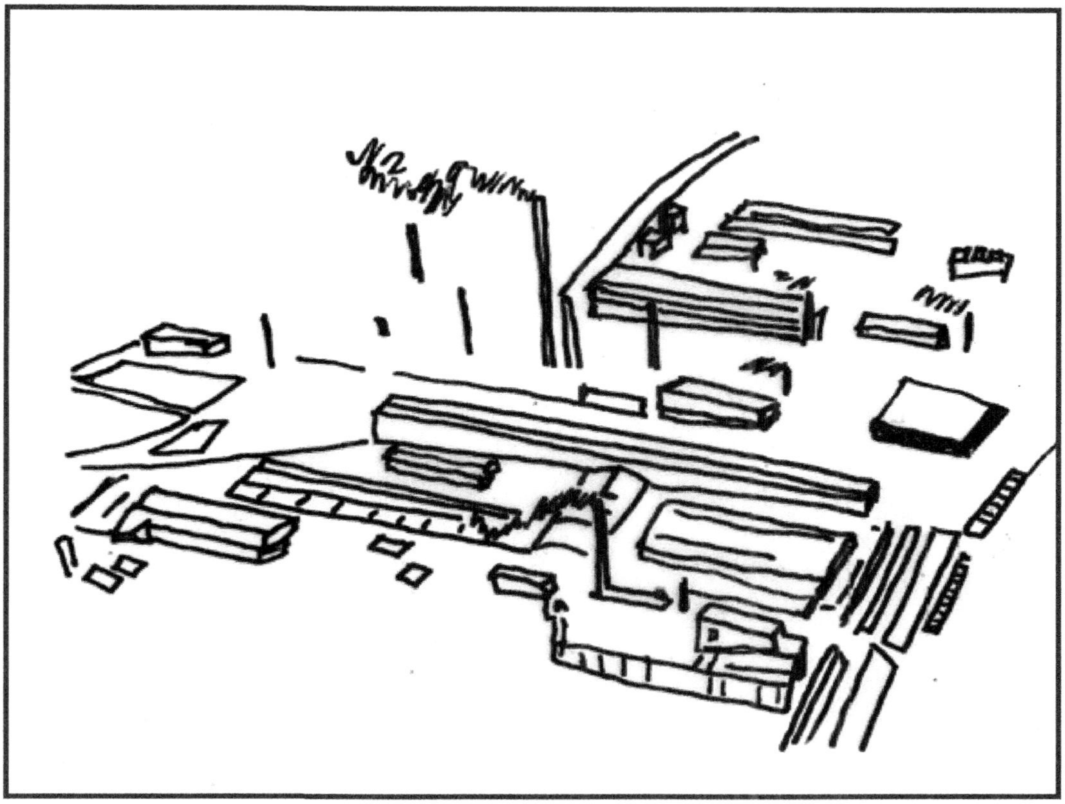

THE POINT TO REMEMBER IS THAT THINGS FOR GERMANY WEREN'T ACTUALLY ALL THAT BAD ECONOMICALLY. THE COUNTRY RETAINED THE POSSIBILITY OF RISING UP AGAIN IN THE FUTURE. AFTER ALL, IT HADN'T BEEN PARTITIONED BY THE ALLIES, AND IT KEPT NEARLY 90 PERCENT OF ITS ECONOMIC RESOURCES.

Gott in Himmel! If one day we manage to shake off the Versailles Treaty and rearm, *we're potentially stronger* than we were in 1914!
STRATEGICALLY, THINGS WEREN'T SO BAD EITHER.
Yes, and even after WWII, when spli- in two, Germany came back to be the number one power in Europe.

TO THE EAST OF GERMANY WAS NO LONGER HUGE RUSSIA BUT A NUMBER OF WEAK STATES. THESE SO-CALLED "SUCCESSOR STATES" HAD ONE THING IN COMMON: NONE HAD ETHNIC UNIFORMITY AND NONE AGREED WITH THE BORDERS IT HAD BEEN GIVEN AFTER THE WAR. THESE STATES COULD THEORETICALLY ONE DAY BE TAKEN OVER BY GERMANY AND BE USED BY GERMANS AS "LIVING SPACE".

LET'S NOT FORGET THE HUGE PSYCHOLOGICAL EFFECT THE TREATY OF BREST-LITOVSK MUST HAVE HAD ON THE GERMANS DURING THE SHORT PERIOD IT WAS IN EFFECT FROM MARCH TO NOVEMBER, 1918.

What the Treaty of Brest-Litovsk took from Russia in March, 1918.

A lot of Germans must've been salivating at all that fertile Ukrainian land, all those mineral deposits and vast resources that had briefly belonged to Germany.
THE BIG PROBLEM FOR THE WEIMAR REPUBLIC WASN'T ECONOMIC BUT RATHER POLITICAL.

POLITICAL DEMORALIZATION AND A SENSE OF "NATIONAL SHAME" GUARANTEED CONSTANT RIGHT-WING OPPOSITION TO THE S.P.D GOVERNMENT IN BERLIN .

The government's a gang of villains.
And you're angels?

AS 1919 DREW TO A CLOSE, THE ATMOSPHERE IN THE COUNTRY WAS ONE OF **DOOM**.

NO ONE BELIEVED THAT THE REPUBLIC AND ITS GOVERNMENT WOULD LAST ANOTHER 6 MONTHS.

THEN, IN FEBRUARY 1920, AS IF DELIBERATELY TRYING TO MAKE THE GERMAN POT BOIL OVER, THE ALLIES PRESENTED A LIST OF 900 GERMANS THEY DEMANDED BE SURRENDERED FOR TRIAL AS WAR CRIMINALS.

The list included almost every German who'd played any important role in the war: generals, politicians, and officers!

GENERAL HANS VON SEECKT, WHO BECAME CHIEF OF THE GERMAN ARMY AFTER THE TREATY OF VERSAILLES WAS SIGNED, TOLD HIS OFFICERS THAT IF PRESIDENT EBERT'S S.P.D GOVERNMENT WOULDN'T OPPOSE THE ALLIED DEMANDS, THE ARMY CERTAINLY WOULD!

No future order from the Inter-Allied Control Commission demanding the destruction of our army will be complied with!

General Hans von Seeckt

FROM NOW ON THE GERMAN ARMY WOULD ONLY BE REDUCED ON PAPER.

THERE WAS A TREMENDOUS **MOOD OF DEFIANCE** AMONG THE GENERAL PUBLIC AND THE MILITARY.

THE **INTER-ALLIED CONTROL COMMISSION** WAS THE "WATCHDOG" OF THE TREATY OF VERSAILLES. IT MADE SURE THE GERMANS DID WHAT THE TREATY TOLD THEM TO DO.

Ha, **fat** chance!

THINGS BECAME TENSE IN FEBRUARY 1920 WHEN THE COMMISSION ORDERED THE DISPERSAL OF TWO *FREIKORPS* UNITS IN BERLIN.

THESE TWO BRIGADES - TWELVE THOUSAND MEN IN ALL - WERE STATIONED AT A MILITARY CAMP A FEW MILES OUTSIDE BERLIN.

LEADING THE *FREIKORPS* MEN WERE EXTREMIST CONSERVATIVES UNDER **GENERAL LUDENDORFF: DR. WOLFGANG KAPP**, A RIGHT-WING JOURNALIST, **CAPTAIN WALDEMAR PABST** (REMEMBER HIS ROLE IN THE ASSASSINATION OF ROSA LUXEMBURG AND KARL LIEBKNECHT), AND **GENERAL WALTHER LUTTWITZ**, WHO'D COMMANDED THE OPERATIONS AGAINST THE SPARTACIST-COMMUNISTS DURING THEIR FAILED REVOLUTION IN JANUARY 1919.

Dr. Wolfgang Kapp — Captain Waldemar Pabst — General Walther Luttwitz

ON THE NIGHT OF MARCH 12-13, THE 12,000 FREIKORPS MEN SET OUT ON THE 12-MILE MARCH TO BERLIN TO TOPPLE THE GOVERNMENT.

AT DAWN, AS THE UNITS WERE NEARING THE CAPITAL, THE HEAD OF THE ARMY, GENERAL SEECKT, COLDLY INFORMED DEFENCE MINISTER NOSKE THAT THE REGULAR ARMY WOULDN'T DEFEND THE S.P.D GOVERNMENT AGAINST THESE *FREIKORPS* UNITS. HE SAID THAT THE REGULAR ARMY WOULD STAY IN THEIR BARRACKS AND REMAIN STRICTLY NEUTRAL.

There can be no question of ordering the *Reichswehr* to fight against the Free Corps! The *Reichswehr* won't fire on the *Reichswehr*!

General Seeckt

Gee, he just equated the right-wing fanatics of the *Freikorps* with the army! The guy identifies with the bastards!
RADICAL F RON TODAY

LET'S KEEP IN MIND THAT AT LEAST 20 PERCENT OF THE OFFICERS IN THE GERMAN ARMY WERE STILL ARISTOCRAT *JUNKERS*, AND THEY ABSOLUTELY HATED EBERT'S SOCIAL DEMOCRATIC REPUBLIC.

The feeling of the army towards the government was lukewarm. It stood beside the government, but not behind it.

President Ebert

NOSKE FELT TERRIBLY BETRAYED.
This night has shown me the bankruptcy of my policy. My faith in the officer corps is shattered. It's deserted me. There's nothing for me but suicide.
Noske didn't kill himself. He resigned as Defense Minister and accepted a lesser position.

WHEN THE *FREIKORPS* UNITS REACHED BERLIN, THEY TOOK UP POSITIONS AND CALLED THE PEOPLE TO JOIN THEM IN OVERTHROWING THE GOVERNMENT. WHEN THAT DIDN'T HAPPEN, THEY SAID THAT WOLFGANG KAPP WAS NOW CHANCELLOR.

THE NATIONAL GOVERNMENT FLED TO STUTTGART AND PRESIDENT EBERT CALLED FOR A **GENERAL STRIKE** AGAINST THE *PUTSCH* (THIS ODD WORD MEANS A SECRETLY PLOTTED AND SUDDENLY EXECUTED ATTEMPT BY A GROUP TO OVERTHROW A GOVERNMENT).

THE PEOPLE OF BERLIN SAVED THE DAY FOR THE REPUBLIC BY SHOWING THEIR SUPPORT FOR THE GOVERNMENT AND GOING OUT INTO THE STREETS AND STRIKING.

What's a general strike?
Dude, that's when you wake up in the morning and switch on the lights but there's no electricity, turn on the water but it doesn't run, call a friend, but the phone doesn't work...
Not even if it's a cell phone?
Not even...and no buses or taxis run, and all the stores are closed, and...well...basically no one works. Life's pretty hard when no one works.

THE STRIKE MEANT THAT NO OFFICIAL STATEMENTS COULD BE PUBLISHED BY DR. KAPP AND HIS *FREIKORPS* SUPPORTERS.

UNABLE TO GET THE SUPPORT OF THE GENERAL PUBLIC, THE KAPP GOVERNMENT COLLAPSED AFTER JUST FOUR DAYS, ON MARCH 17, 1920.

...DR. KAPP ESCAPED BY PLANE TO SWEDEN.

The failure of the Kapp Putsch didn't mean the end of the glorious *Freikors!*

MANY *FREIKORPS* MEMBERS FLED TO THE STATE OF BAVARIA WHERE THE LOCAL GOVERNMENT OF RIGHT-WING MONARCHIST **GUSTAV VON KAHR** WARMLY WELCOMED THEM.

Bavaria's the natural place to be for anyone who wants to rid Germany of the Traitor Weimar Republic.

Gustav von Kahr

INSPIRED BY THE GENERAL STRIKE DURING THE KAPP PUTSCH, A WORKERS' UPRISING BEGAN IN THE RUHR REGION OF GERMANY.
THE UPRISING WASN'T SUCCESSFUL AND WAS PUT DOWN BY THE REGULAR ARMY AND THE *FREIKORPS*.
Like the January revolution in 1919, the SPD government is again on the side of the right-wing *Freikorps*!
THE GOVERNMENT'S REPRESSION OF THE 1920 RUHR WORKERS' UPRISING BECAME A MAJOR SOURCE OF CONFLICT WITHIN THE SOCIALIST MOVEMENT.
This division within the ranks of the left weakened the only group in Germany which could've stood up to the Nazis in the future.
I disagree. How can you count people like Ebert and many members of the SPD as true socialists? It was impossible for these people to see eye-to-eye with the communists or the radical socialists in the USPD!

OTHER WORKER REBELLIONS WERE CRUSHED IN MARCH 1921 IN SAXONY AND HAMBURG.
THE FAR RIGHT IN GERMANY WAS VERY STRONG AND ACTIVE. IMMEDIATELY AFTER THE WAR ENDED IT WAS DOMINATED BY MONARCHISTS. HOWEVER, THE YOUNGER, AND MORE RADICAL, GENERATION SUPPORTED *VÖLKISCH* NATIONALISM AND DIDN'T WANT TO BRING THE *KAISER* BACK TO GERMANY.
Völkisch ...what?
Völkisch nationalism, from "*volk*", a vague term which translates to "people", "nation" and "race". It supports the creation of a "superior" society based on ethnic German "folk" culture and so-called German "blood".

THIS YOUNGER GENERATION WANTED TO DISMANTLE THE WEIMAR REPUBLIC AND CREATE A STRONG NEW STATE BASED UPON A MILITARY-STYLE PHILOSOPHY THAT WOULD REVIVE THE "SPIRIT OF 1914", THAT IS, THE SPIRIT OF NATIONAL UNITY.
That national unity was called ***volksgemeinschaft.***
IT'S IMPORTANT TO KEEP IN MIND THAT THE WEIMAR REPUBLIC WAS HATED BY BOTH THE RIGHT AND THE LEFT.
RIGHT-WINGERS HATED IT AS "SOCIALIST", AND LEFT-WINGERS HATED IT FOR BEING PRO-CAPITALIST AND FOR HAVING WORKED WITH THE RIGHT TO PUT DOWN THE 1919 BERLIN REVOLUTION AND A SERIES OF OTHER REVOLTS AROUND THE COUNTRY.

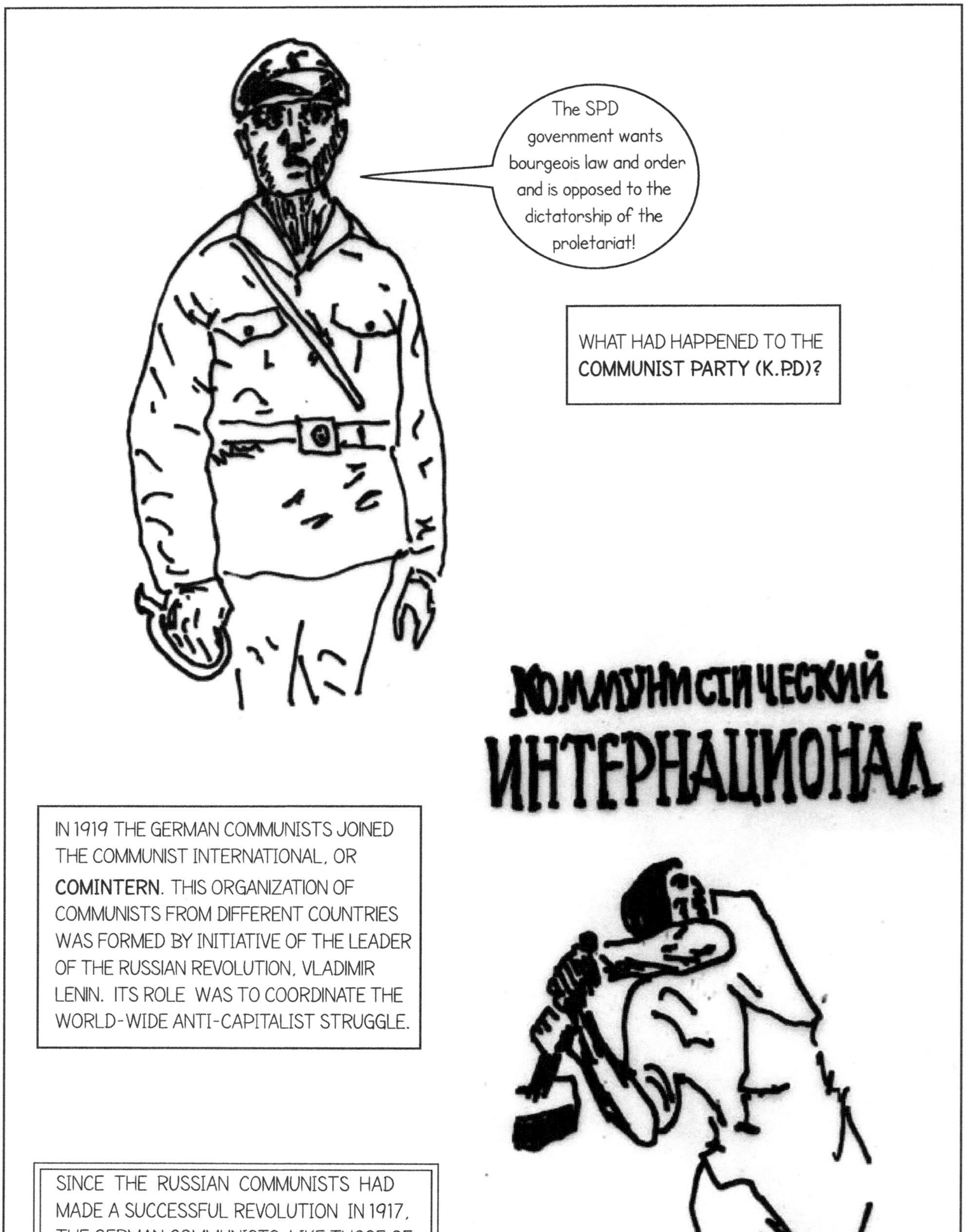
The SPD government wants bourgeois law and order and is opposed to the dictatorship of the proletariat!
WHAT HAD HAPPENED TO THE **COMMUNIST PARTY (K.P.D)?**
КОММУНИСТИЧЕСКИЙ ИНТЕРНАЦИОНАЛ
IN 1919 THE GERMAN COMMUNISTS JOINED THE COMMUNIST INTERNATIONAL, OR **COMINTERN**. THIS ORGANIZATION OF COMMUNISTS FROM DIFFERENT COUNTRIES WAS FORMED BY INITIATIVE OF THE LEADER OF THE RUSSIAN REVOLUTION, VLADIMIR LENIN. ITS ROLE WAS TO COORDINATE THE WORLD-WIDE ANTI-CAPITALIST STRUGGLE.
SINCE THE RUSSIAN COMMUNISTS HAD MADE A SUCCESSFUL REVOLUTION IN 1917, THE GERMAN COMMUNISTS, LIKE THOSE OF MOST OTHER COUNTRIES, LISTENED TO THE RUSSIAN "TEACHERS OF REVOLUTION".

Übt
Solidarität!
mit SowjetRussland

NOT SURPRISINGLY, THE GERMAN COMMUNIST PARTY FELL UNDER MOSCOW'S CONTROL. INITIALLY, THIS WAS FINE (FROM THE POINT OF VIEW OF THOSE WHO REALLY WANTED TO MAKE REVOLUTION). HOWEVER, AS THE RUSSIAN COMMUNISTS BECAME MORE AND MORE CONSERVATIVE UNDER STALIN IN THE 1920S, IT WAS LESS GOOD.

Under Stalin, the Soviet Union has become a bureaucratic state that's not interested in making world revolution.

Leon Trotsky, co-leader with Lenin of the 1917 Russian Revolution.

Ernst Thälmann, Leader of the German Communist Party (KPD)

Here he is again, talking to workers.

IN THE EARLY 1920s THE COMMUNIST PARTY HAD A MEMBERSHIP OF 400,000 AND 33 NEWSPAPERS. ALL THE SAME, THE K.P.D WASN'T A FORCE FOR REVOLUTION. IT WASN'T GOING TO TRY TO SEIZE POWER THE WAY THE SPARTACISTS HAD IN 1919.
The KPD was a failure among the trade unions because of its strictly pro-Soviet stance!
We know what kind of docile trade unions workers in the Soviet Union had under Stalin!

FOR THESE REASONS, THE RIGHT WAS MUCH MORE OF A DANGER TO THE WEIMAR REPUBLIC THAN THE LEFT.

THE RIGHT-WING GOT MOST OF ITS SUPPORT FROM BIG BUSINESSMEN, THE CHURCH, THE CIVIL SERVICE, AND THE LEGAL SYSTEM.

Bring back the *Kaiser*!
German businessmen relaxing.

THE HOSTILITY OF THE LEGAL SYSTEM TO THE WEIMAR DEMOCRACY WAS CLEAR FROM HOW LENIENTLY THE COURTS DEALT WITH RIGHT-WING TERRORISTS. THEY RARELY HANDED DOWN STIFF SENTENCES, AND JUDGES OFTEN EXPRESSED THEIR SYMPATHY WITH THE FANATICAL ANTI-SOCIALISTS.

HITLER ENTERS THE STAGE

WHEN THE SPARTACIST REVOLT WAS BEING CRUSHED IN BERLIN IN 1919, A MAN CALLED **ADOLPH HITLER** WAS IN MUNICH, BAVARIA.

HITLER WAS AN AUSTRIAN CITIZEN.

HE WAS BORN ON APRIL 20, 1889, IN THIS HOUSE IN BRAUNAU AM INN, AN AUSTRIAN TOWN ON THE BORDER WITH GERMANY.

AS A BOY, HE DIDN'T WANT TO BE A CUSTOMS' OFFICIAL LIKE HIS DAD, SO HE DROPPED OUT OF SCHOOL. INSTEAD, HE HOPED TO BE AN ARTIST.

TO PURSUE THIS DREAM, HE MOVED TO **VIENNA** IN 1908, BUT WAS REJECTED BY THE ACADEMY OF FINE ARTS. SO HE TRIED TO MAKE A LIVING AS A WATERCOLOR PAINTER WHO COPIED POSTCARDS AND SOLD THEM TO TOURISTS AS PAINTINGS.

LIKE THIS ONE

It's actually not that bad.

HE WASN'T SUCCESSFUL. WHEN HE RAN OUT OF MONEY HE EVEN LIVED IN THE STREET A WHILE.

HITLER STAYED IN VIENNA FROM 1908 TO 1913. THE AUSTRIAN CAPITAL AT THE TIME WAS A HOTBED OF RELIGIOUS PREJUDICE AND RACISM. FEARS OF BEING OVERRUN BY IMMIGRANTS FROM THE EAST WERE WIDESPREAD. HITLER SHARED THESE BIASES AND FEARS.

Vienna really affected Hitler's *weltanschauung,* as the Germans say, his world view.

IN VIENNA HITLER WAS INFUENCED BY AN AUSTRIAN, GEORG RITTER VON SCHÖNERER. THIS MAN WAS A PAN-GERMANIST. HE WANTED ALL GERMANS INSIDE AND OUTSIDE OF GERMANY TO UNITE. HE ALSO ADVOCATED RADICAL GERMAN NATIONALISM, ANTI-SEMITISM, ANTI-CATHOLICISM, ANTI-SLAVISM AND ANTI-HABSBURG VIEWS.

It's from this guy Schönerer that Hitler'll adopt the *Heil* greeting, the *Führer* title, and the model of absolute party leadership for the future Nazi movement.

HITLER WAS ALSO IMPRESSED WITH THE ANTISEMITISM AND ANTI-LIBERAL AGITATION OF KARL LUEGER. HE WAS THE MAYOR OF VIENNA DURING HIS TIME IN THE AUSTRIAN CAPITAL, AND USED A RABBLE-ROUSING STYLE OF PUBLIC SPEAKING.

UNLIKE VON SCHÖNERER, LUEGER WASN'T A GERMAN NATIONALIST. RATHER, HE WAS A PRO-CATHOLIC SUPPORTER OF THE AUSTRIAN EMPIRE.

WHILE SCHÖNERER WAS MORE AT HOME WITH THE ELITIST NATIONALISM OF UNIVERSITY STUDENT FRATERNITIES, LUEGER WAS COMFORTABLE WITH BIG CITY CROWDS, AND HE COULD CHANNEL THEIR PROTEST INTO POLITICAL GAIN.

IN MAY OF 1913 HITLER MOVED TO MUNICH. HE PROBABLY LEFT VIENNA TO AVOID CONSCRIPTION INTO AUSTRIA'S ARMY. HE HAD ALWAYS SUPPORTED GERMANY OVER HIS NATIVE AUSTRIA, WHICH HE THOUGHT WEAK AND CORRUPT.

HITLER GOT MANY OF HIS IDEAS FROM SCHÖNERER, BUT HIS STRATEGY AND TACTICS FROM LUEGER.

I always hated the mixture of races in the Habsburg Empire.

DID HITLER MANAGE TO HIDE FROM THE AUSTRIAN ARMY?

NO...THEY CAUGHT UP WITH HIM IN MUNICH...

WHEN THE AUSTRIAN ARMY DOCTORS GAVE HIM A MEDICAL EXAMINATION, THEY DISCOVERED THAT HE HAD A HEALTH PROBLEM, AND DEEMED HIM UNFIT FOR MILITARY SERVICE.

What kind of health problem did Hitler have?
When we examined him, hmmm, we found that he had an elevated testicle.
Wow, back then army doctors must've been a lot stricter than nowadays.
HITLER WANTED TO SERVE IN THE ARMY, ONLY NOT THE AUSTRIAN ARMY. HE WAS VERY EXCITED THE WAR HAD COME. NOW HE COULD FINALLY PROVE HIMSELF AND STOP LIVING THE LIFE OF A LONELY LOSER. SO HE VOLUNTEERED TO SERVE IN A BAVARIAN REGIMENT, THE 16TH (ALSO CALLED REGIMENT LIST AFTER ITS FIRST COMMANDER). HE WAS ACCEPTED WITHOUT A THOROUGH MEDICAL EXAM.

Here's Hitler in the crowd in Munich, when the war was announced on August 3, 1914. He was 25 years old.

NOT TOO CLEAR? HERE'S A CLOSE-UP.

Hitler (on the right) poses with two war buddies.

DURING WORLD WAR ONE, HITLER WAS A TRENCH "RUNNER", WHICH WAS VERY DANGEROUS BECAUSE HE HAD TO CARRY INFORMATION FROM ONE COMMAND POST TO ANOTHER UNDER ENEMY FIRE.

HITLER WAS TWICE DECORATED WITH THE IRON CROSS, THE ARMY'S TOP MEDAL FOR BRAVERY.

DESPITE HIS BRAVERY, HITLER'S SUPERIORS DIDN'T THINK HE HAD LEADERSHIP QUALITIES, SO HE WASN'T PROMOTED BEYOND THE LOWLY RANK OF *GEFREITER* (SOMETHING LIKE LANCE CORPORAL IN ENGLISH).

Hey, that's not fair, you don't know this for a fact! Maybe Hitler wasn't promoted because his commanders wanted to keep him as a runner, since he was so good at it.

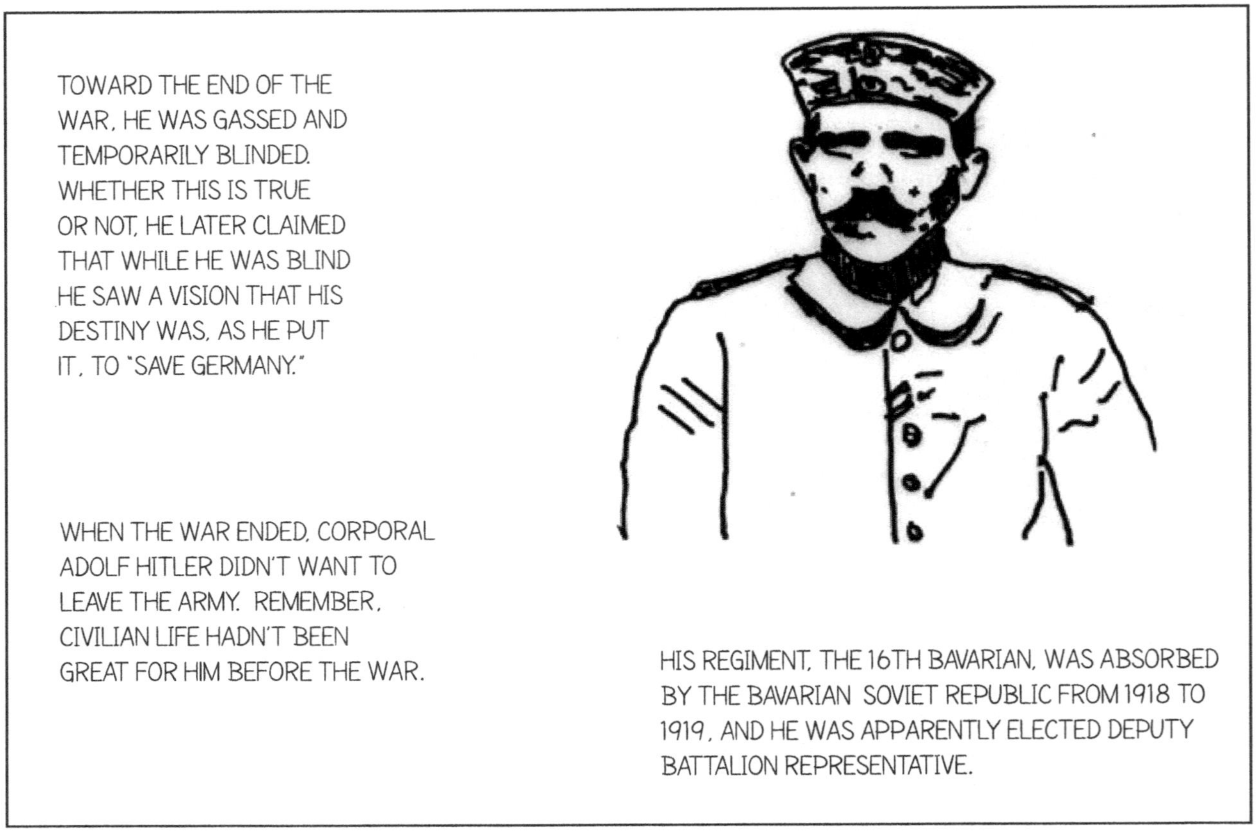
TOWARD THE END OF THE WAR, HE WAS GASSED AND TEMPORARILY BLINDED. WHETHER THIS IS TRUE OR NOT, HE LATER CLAIMED THAT WHILE HE WAS BLIND HE SAW A VISION THAT HIS DESTINY WAS, AS HE PUT IT, TO "SAVE GERMANY."
WHEN THE WAR ENDED, CORPORAL ADOLF HITLER DIDN'T WANT TO LEAVE THE ARMY. REMEMBER, CIVILIAN LIFE HADN'T BEEN GREAT FOR HIM BEFORE THE WAR.
HIS REGIMENT, THE 16TH BAVARIAN, WAS ABSORBED BY THE BAVARIAN SOVIET REPUBLIC FROM 1918 TO 1919, AND HE WAS APPARENTLY ELECTED DEPUTY BATTALION REPRESENTATIVE.

ACCORDING TO HISTORIAN THOMAS WEBER, HITLER EVEN ATTENDED THE FUNERAL OF COMMUNIST KURT EISNER (WHO WAS A GERMAN JEW), WEARING A BLACK MOURNING ARMBAND ON ONE ARM AND A RED COMMUNIST ARMBAND ON THE OTHER.
If this story's true, that's evidence that Hitler's political beliefs hadn't yet solidified, and at that time supported the idea of a classless society and was anti-monarchist.
More speculation! The picture I've seen has Hitler standing on a sidewalk as the Eisner funeral procession walks past. He doesn't look like a participant, just an onlooker. And how on Earth can you tell one armband was red when the photo was - as they all were back then - black-and-white?

HITLER OF COURSE NEVER MENTIONED ANY SERVICE WITH THE BAVARIAN SOVIET REPUBLIC. WE KNOW HE SAID THAT HE BECAME AN ANTISEMITE IN 1913 IN VIENNA. THIS VIEW'S BEEN QUESTIONED BY SOME HISTORIANS, WHO ARGUE THAT HE PROBABLY WASN'T A FANATICAL ANTISEMITE YET.

Well, what is it? Was he an anti-Semite in 1919 or wasn't he? And had he flirted with communism?
The honest answer is we don't know for sure.

IT'S CONCEIVABLE THAT HITLER ALTERED HIS POLITICAL VIEWS IN RESPONSE TO THE TREATY OF VERSAILLES OF JUNE 1919, AND THAT IT WAS THEN THAT HE BECAME AN ANTISEMITIC GERMAN NATIONALIST. BUT WE DON'T HAVE THE EVIDENCE TO PROVE IT.

AS A NAZI, HITLER HAD EXPRESSED OPPOSITION TO CAPITALISM; HE REGARDED IT AS HAVING JEWISH ORIGINS, AND ACCUSED CAPITALISM OF HOLDING NATIONS TO RANSOM IN THE SELFISH INTERESTS OF A PARASITIC CLASS OF RENTIERS.

A class of…what?
Rentiers - people who get their income from *rentes;* that's French for investments. Speculators, in plain English.

SOON AFTER THE WAR ENDED, CORPORAL ADOLF HITLER ENLISTED AS AN INFORMER-PROPAGANDIST EMPLOYED BY THE ARMY'S SPECIAL PROPAGANDA COMMANDO AT AN ARMY BASE OUTSIDE MUNICH.
A professional rat, to put it bluntly!
Anton Drexler
HIS TASK WAS TO **SPY** ON POLITICAL ORGANIZATIONS.
ONE DAY HITLER WALKED INTO THE OFFICES OF THE GERMAN WORKERS' PARTY, THE ***DEUTSCHE ARBEITER PARTEI*** **(D.A.P).**
THIS PARTY HAD BEEN FOUNDED IN 1919 BY A POLITICALLY AMBITIOUS RAILWAY LOCKSMITH CALLED **ANTON DREXLER.**
With a name like German Workers' Party, Hitler probably expected to find Communists in the DAP.

PROBABLY TO HIS OWN SURPRISE, HITLER LIKED WHAT THEY PREACHED AT THE D.A.P - A BIZARRE BLEND OF ANTI-CAPITALISM, ANTI-SOCIALISM, FAITH IN THE GERMAN *VOLK*, ANTI-SEMITISM, EXTREMIST NATIONALISM, AND BELIEF THAT EVERYTHING IN LIFE IS BASED ON THE RACE THAT A PERSON HAPPENS TO BELONG TO.

THE BOSS AT THE GERMAN WORKERS' PARTY, ANTON DREXLER, WAS VERY IMPRESSED BY HITLER, WHO WAS INTENSE AND PASSIONATE AND ALWAYS SAID PATRIOTIC THINGS ABOUT GERMANY (EVEN THOUGH, OR MAYBE *BECAUSE* HE WAS A CITIZEN OF AUSTRIA).

DREXLER SAW THAT HITLER HAD A TALENT FOR PUBLIC SPEAKING SO HE ARRANGED TO HAVE HIM TRAINED.

Race? That doesn't take into account what kind of a person someone is, how they behave, whether they're good or bad, or whether they earn an honest living.

HITLER'S TALENTS WERE REFINED, AND HE WAS TAUGHT HOW TO DRESS PROPERLY AND ACT IMPORTANT LIKE A POLITICIAN.

SOON HITLER BEGAN TO DOMINATE THE **D.A.P.**, WHICH WAS RENAMED **NATIONAL SOCIALIST GERMAN WORKERS' PARTY (N.S.D.A.P), OR "NAZI" PARTY,** FROM A SHORTENING OF THE FIRST TWO LETTERS ("S" IS PRONOUNCED "Z" IN GERMAN WHEN IT COMES BEFORE A VOWEL; THE WORD NAZI IS SPELLED JUST THE WAY IT SOUNDS).

BUT LET'S LEAVE HITLER FOR NOW. APART FROM A SMALL GROUP OF PEOPLE IN MUNICH, FEW KNEW OR CARED ABOUT HIM...YET.

THE TROUBLED EARLY 1920s

WE'VE SEEN THAT DESPITE DEFEAT IN WORLD WAR ONE, GERMANY HAD THE FOUNDATIONS (FACTORIES AND INFRA-STRUCTURE) TO BE THE ECONOMIC MOTOR OF EUROPE.

PRESIDENT EBERT AND HIS COLLEAGUES IN THE SOCIAL DEMOCRATIC GOVERNMENT HOPED THAT IF THEY MANAGED TO SURVIVE THE POLITICAL STORMS AT HOME, THEN ALL WOULD TURN OUT FINE IN THE END.

Weathering the political tensions in Germany wasn't made easy by the Allies, especially France!

BUT THINGS DIDN'T TURN OUT THAT WAY...

WHEN THE GERMANS HEARD, IN APRIL OF 1921, THAT THE REPARATIONS BILL THEY HAD TO PAY WAS 132 BILLION GOLD MARKS (ABOUT 31.5 BILLION DOLLARS), THEY WERE FURIOUS!

This is Crazy!

THEIR ANGER WAS MADE EVEN MORE INTENSE BECAUSE FINANCE MINISTER **MATTHIAS ERZBERGER** (WHO HAD SIGNED THE ARMISTICE IN 1918 AND WAS THOUGHT TO BE A "TRAITOR" BY MANY) WANTED TO TAX WAR PROFITS AND INHERITED WEALTH.

What's wrong with a tax on war profits and inherited wealth?
RADICAL PERSON FROM TODAY

We Communists believe that one of the first measures of a truly socialist government isn't to tax inherited wealth, but to make it *illegal!*

Vladimir Lenin

THE SITUATION FOR THE GOVERNMENT CONTINUTED TO GET MORE DIFFICLT AS RIGHT-WING FANATICS KEPT UP THE PRESSURE AND CRITICIZED IT FOR ALL OF GERMANY'S MANY PROBLEMS.

THE PRESSURE FROM THE RIGHT BECAME EVEN MORE INTENSE AFTER MAY 1921, WHEN GERMANY'S STUBBORN POLICY OF OBSTRUCTION CHANGED UNDER THE NEW CHANCELLOR, **JOSEPH WIRTH** (MAY 1921-NOVEMBER 1922) TO ONE OF SO-CALLED ***ERFULLINGSPOLITIK*** OR "FULFILLMENT".

Germany has no choice but to fulfill its obligations to the Allies. Otherwise, they'll really make our lives miserable.

Chancellor Joseph Wirth

THIS APPARENT COOPERATION WITH THE ALLIES MADE THE RIGHT VERY ANGRY. AS A RESULT, THERE WAS A LOT OF POLITICAL VIOLENCE IN DIFFERENT PARTS OF GERMANY.

Mathias Erzburger

IN AUGUST OF 1921 ERZBERGER WAS MURDERED BY A RIGHT-WING FANATIC.

AS WITH OTHER CASES OF POLITICAL VIOLENCE BY THE RIGHT, THE JUDGES TREATED THE PERPETRATORS WITH KID GLOVES AND DIDN'T PUNISH THEM STRICTLY.

Many judges are on the side of the right-wing assassins!

SO LONG AS THE INTER-ALLIED CONTROL COMMISSION REMAINED IN GERMANY, THERE WERE LIMITS TO WHAT GERMANY'S MILITARY LEADERS COULD DO, NO MATTER HOW WELL THEY HID THESE ACTIVITIES, OR HOW MANY "TRAITORS" THEY KILLED...

FACED WITH THIS SITUATION, THE HEAD OF THE GERMAN ARMY, GENERAL SEECKT, BEGAN TO LOOK AROUND FOR A COUNTRY WITH A SIMILAR INTEREST TO GERMANY'S IN DEFYING THE ALLIES. THERE WAS ONLY ONE LOGICAL CHOICE - BOLSHEVIK RUSSIA.

We really hate Communists, but the *Reichswehr* entered into negotiations with the Red Army in 1921.

THE GERMAN ARMY NEEDED TO BE ABLE SECRETLY TO BUILD, TRAIN, AND EXPERIMENT WITH WEAPONS FORBIDDEN TO IT UNDER THE VERSAILLES TREATY. IN RETURN FOR THESE, IT WAS WILLING TO GIVE THE SOVIET UNION THE BENEFIT OF GERMAN MILITARY TECHNIQUES AND MANUFACTURING PROCESSES.

NEGOTIATIONS BETWEEN THE GERMAN MILITARY AND THE RED ARMY LED TO THE DIPLOMATIC REVOLUTION OF THE **TREATY OF RAPALLO OF 1922.**

SIGNED IN RAPALLO, ITALY, ON APRIL 16, 1922, THIS TREATY SHOCKED THE ALLIES BECAUSE THE TWO PARIAHS OF EUROPE - GERMANY AND RUSSIA - DECIDED JOINTLY TO BREAK THE ALLIED BOYCOTT ISOLATING THEM. THEY ALSO AGREED TO ABANDON ANY FINANCIAL CLAIMS WHICH EACH MIGHT BRING AGAINST THE OTHER FOLLOWING THE GREAT WAR.

The *Reichswehr* set up a front company called "Corporation for the Furtherance of Trade Enterprises" that pretended to promote trade with the Soviet Union.
GERMAN SOLDIERS WERE PERMITTED TO TRAIN IN SECRET IN THE SOVIET UNION AND BUILD VARIOUS MILITARY INSTALLATIONS THERE, INCLUDING A POISON GAS FACTORY, AND PLANTS THAT MADE TANKS, ARMORED VEHICLES AND SHELLS. THEY ALSO HAD AN AIR BASE TO TRAIN PILOTS AND TEST PLANES.
Wow.
LIKE THESE HEINKEL D 17s AT THE *REICHSWEHR'S* FLIGHT SCHOOL IN LIPETZK IN THE SOUTH OF RUSSIA:

Walter Rathenau

WALTHER RATHENAU, THE INDUSTRIALIST AND DIPLOMAT WHO NEGOTIATED THE LOCARNO TREATY FOR GERMANY, WAS MURDERED BY RIGHT-WINGERS IN JUNE OF 1922 BECAUSE HE WAS A JEW.

I guess for the right-wingers who killed him, his being Jewish outweighed the benefit that the German army got from his idea. How stupid!

THE FRENCH IN THE MEANTIME WERE WORRIED AND DEPRESSED. BY 1920 THE BASES OF THEIR SECURITY SET BY THE TREATY OF VERSAILLES HAD DISAPPEARED. THIS WAS BECAUSE AMERICA HAD PULLED OUT OF EUROPE AND WAS ACTING ISOLATIONIST, AND BRITAIN DIDN'T WANT TO PRESSURE THE GERMANS TO PAY REPARATIONS.

The Germans are increasingly unwilling to pay reparations. They say they don't have the money, but I smell a rat. The government in Berlin's making their economic situation look worse than it really is!

THE FRENCH ACTUALLY MET THE GERMANS HALFWAY DURING THE WIESBADEN AGREEMENTS IN OCTOBER 1921. THEY AGREED TO ACCEPT A PORTION OF REPARATIONS IN KIND, THAT IS, RAW MATERIALS AND INDUSTRIAL PRODUCTS.

...but the German government allowed even these shipments to fall behind.

FRANCE'S TOUGH PRIME MINISTER, **RAYMOND POINCARÉ**, WASN'T GOING TO TAKE NO FROM THE GERMANS ANYMORE.

Ca suffit, enough! I choose confrontation with the Germans! They must do as the Treaty of Versailles says, or else!

French PM Raymond Poincaré

A MAJOR CRISIS BROKE OUT IN NOVEMBER 1922. FOR A THIRD TIME IN THREE YEARS, GERMANY ASKED FOR HER PAYMENTS TO BE SUSPENDED...AND FRANCE HAD SIMPLY HAD ENOUGH...THIS WAS THE DROP THAT OVERFLOWED THE FRENCH CUP!

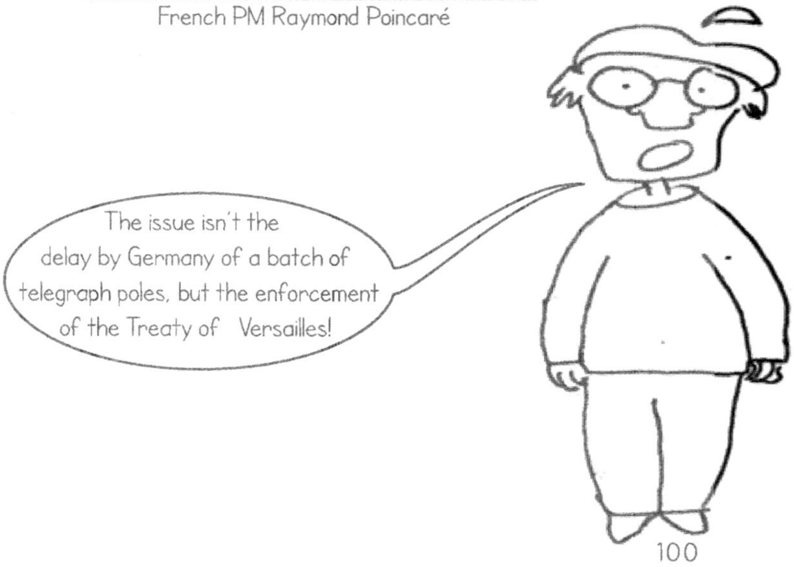
The issue isn't the delay by Germany of a batch of telegraph poles, but the enforcement of the Treaty of Versailles!

IN JANUARY 1923, FRANCE, WITH SUPPORT FROM BELGIUM AND ITALY, SENT FIVE DIVISIONS ACROSS THE RHINE RIVER (GERMANY'S WESTERN BORDER) TO OCCUPY THE INDUSTRIAL AREA OF THE **RUHR.**
Hey, isn't that a violation of the Treaty of Versailles? Isn'- invasion of another country's territory supposed to be illegal!
Yeah, sure, but who's going to stop the French after all they suffered from the Germans in the War?
THE FRENCH AND BELGIANS WANTED TO MAKE SURE THE GERMANS DELIVERED THE RAW MATERIALS THEY'D PROMISED.

LIKE THESE COAL BRIQUETTES THIS FRENCH SOLDIER'S GUARDING.

THIS OF COURSE WAS A VIOLATION OF THE TREATY OF VERSAILLES, AND IT MADE FRANCE LOOK LIKE A BULLY.

THE BRITISH AND AMERICANS WERE FURIOUS...
BUT THE FRENCH WOULDN'T LISTEN.

We'll passively resist!

Chancellor Wilhelm Cuno

THE CHANCELLOR IN GERMANY AT THE TIME WAS A MAN NAMED **WILHELM CUNO**. HE CALLED ON THE POPULATION OF THE RUHR TO USE **"PASSIVE RESISTANCE"** AGAINST THE VERSAILLES TREATY AND THE FOREIGN TROOPS IN THE COUNTRY.

I won't submit!

We're on strike, and I want to see how the French can mine our coal with bayonets.
GERMAN WORKER

CUNO NOT ONLY ENCOURAGED THE RUHR WORKERS TO STRIKE, BUT ORDERED THE GOVERNMENT TO PRINT MONEY SO AS TO GO ON PAYING THEIR WAGES. THE RESULT WASN'T SURPRISING: THE VALUE OF THE MARK FELL EVEN FURTHER.

THERE WAS **INSANE HYPERINFLATION!**

	GERMAN MARKS NEEDED TO BUY ONE OUNCE OF GOLD
JAN 1919	170
SEP 1919	499
JAN 1920	1,340
SEP 1921	2,175
JAN 1922	3,976
SEP 1922	30,381
JAN 1923	372,477
SEP 1923	269,439,000
OCT 1923	347,070,000,000
NOV 1923	7,000,000,000,000

TENSIONS WERE VERY HIGH. THE *FREIKORPS* IGNORED CHANCELLOR CUNO'S ORDER FOR STRICTLY PASSIVE RESISTANCE, AND THERE WERE A NUMBER OF TERRORIST ATTACKS ON FOREIGN TROOPS, WHO HIT BACK AT THE DEMONSTRATING GERMANS.

WHO BENEFITED FROM ALL THE CHEAP MONEY IN 1923?

REICHSBANKNOTE 49p·155586
Fünfzig Millionen Mark
REICHSBANKDIREKTORIUM

BUSINESSMEN NOW FOUND IT VERY INEXPENSIVE TO RUN THEIR COMPANIES AND TO PAY WAGES.

LANDOWNERS ALSO BENEFITED BECAUSE THEIR MORTGAGES (MONEY THEY BORROWED FROM BANKS AGAINST THE VALUE OF THEIR REAL ESTATE) WERE NOW A LOT EASIER TO PAY OFF.

Who do *I* think benefited? The same people who always benefit from the misfortunes of the little guy!

German children playing with stacks of worthless money.

THE PEOPLE HIT HARDEST BY HYPERINFLATION WERE THOSE WITH SAVINGS AND ON FIXED INCOMES, PEOPLE WHOSE WAGES WERE PAID IN WORTHLESS PAPER.

By October 1923, the weekly wage of a skilled worker is barely enough to buy a sack of potatoes.
GERMAN WORKER

RIGHT-WING PROPAGANDISTS BLAMED THE HYPERINFLATION NOT ON THOSE WHO WERE ACTUALLY RESPONSIBLE FOR IT, THAT IS, THE GOVERNMENT IN BERLIN. INSTEAD, THEY BLAMED THE ALLIES, DEMOCRACY, AND...

Don't forget to blame us Jews, too!

THE DECLINE OF GERMANY'S CURRENCY HAD BEGUN *BEFORE* THE WAR ENDED.

The *Kaiser's* government had refused to pay for the war through taxes. And when it ended and the Social Democrats came to power, rather than taxing the industrialists and those who made vast profits from the war, they just printed money!

IN 1923 THE NUMBER OF PEOPLE ON THE DOLE IN GERMANY WAS THREE TIMES THAT OF 1913. THIS MADE THEM CYNICAL AND ALIENATED. MOST GERMANS TRULY BELIEVED THAT DEMOCRACY WAS A SHORT ROAD TO NATIONAL HUMILIATION AND ECONOMIC DISASTER.

TRADE UNIONS SUFFERED BECAUSE THEY COULDN'T TAKE CARE OF THEIR MEMBERS. AS A RESULT, THERE WAS A BIG DROP IN THE MEMBERSHIP AND POLITICAL INFLUENCE OF THE UNIONS.

AS THE RUHR CRISIS WORE ON, FRENCH PREMIER **POINCARÉ** HAD A CLEVER IDEA.

Why don't our unemployed Frenchmen and Belgians operate the Ruhr mines, furnaces and railways!
THIS IDEA WAS IMMEDIATELY VERY POPULAR IN FRANCE AND BELGIUM!

Raymond Poincaré

UNABLE TO DEAL WITH THE CRISIS, THE CUNO GOVERNMENT RESIGNED IN AUGUST OF 1923.

THE SITUATION WAS DESPERATE. THE GERMAN CURRENCY HAD BASICALLY COLLAPSED, AND A SEPARATIST MOVEMENT FOR AN INDEPENDENT RHINELAND HAD EMERGED (IT HAD THE SUPPORT AND BACKING OF THE FRENCH). THERE WAS A REAL THREAT THAT GERMANY MIGHT BREAK UP INTO MANY DIFFERENT STATES, AND RETURN TO THE SITUATION BEFORE IT UNITED BACK IN 1871!

A NEW GOVERNMENT WAS FORMED IN BERLIN WITH A MAN CALLED **GUSTAV STRESEMANN** AS CHANCELLOR.

TO DEAL WITH THE DIFFICULT SITUATION, STRESSEMAN ANNOUNCED, ON SEPTEMBER 26, 1923, THE END OF PASSIVE RESISTANCE.

We must do as the French say or we're *lost*!

Gustav Stresemann

WHAT WAS THE RESULT OF THE 1923 RUHR CRISIS?

ON THE SURFACE, THE FRENCH SEEMED TO HAVE WON. IN REALITY, THOUGH, FRENCH PREMIER POINCARÉ HAD INCREASED THE MISTRUST OF THE ALLIES. THE BRITISH AND THE AMERICANS WERE ESPECIALLY FURIOUS WITH THE FRENCH BEHAVIOR, WHICH THEY BELIEVED THREATENED THE BALANCE OF POWER...AND PEACE IN EUROPE.

Poincaré got us French politically isolated!

ANY FUTURE CO-OPERATION BETWEEN GERMANY AND FRANCE WAS NOW PRACTICALLY IMPOSSIBLE.
IN FRANCE BOTH THE LEFT AND THE RIGHT CRITICIZED POINCARÉ.
Poincaré didn't seize the opportunity in the crisis to break the unity of Germany and her economic backbone, the Ruhr.
Right-winger
His high-handed action in the Ruhr served the selfish interests of French capitalists.
Left-winger
THE LESSON THE FRENCH LEARNED FROM THE RUHR CRISIS OF 1923 WAS NEVER AGAIN TRY AND PUNISH GERMANY ON THEIR OWN. POINCARÉ'S ACTION HAD ISOLATED FRANCE AND MADE HER WEAKER DIPLOMATICALLY.
MOREOVER, FRANCE HERSELF HAD SUFFERED ECONOMICALLY DURING THE CRISIS AS THE FRANC HAD FALLEN IN VALUE.
The French now understand they were naïve to think they could act in a unilateral way.
BEFORE WE TURN TO SEE WHAT ADOLF HITLER WAS UP TO, A FEW WORDS ARE IN ORDER ABOUT **CULTURE** IN THE WEIMAR REPUBLIC.

CULTURE IN THE WEIMAR REPUBLIC

THE 1920s SAW A REMARKABLE **CULTURAL RENAISSANCE** IN GERMANY.

THIS WAS NOT ALL POSITIVE....
Would you believe it, clubs and bars were full during the worst phase of the hyperinflation of 1923!

AT A TIME WHEN MONEY WAS LOSING VALUE FAST, NIGHT CLUBS WERE FULL OF SPECULATORS WHO SPENT THEIR DAILY PROFITS SO THEY WOULDN'T LOSE THE VALUE THE NEXT DAY.
The people in these establishments weren't ordinary workers.

BERLIN INTELLECTUALS CONDEMNED CAPITALISM, AND DEMANDED RADICAL CHANGES ON THE CULTURAL SCENE.

Soviet poet and playwright, Vladimir Mayakovsky

Mein Gott! Young women are being Americanised! They're wearing makeup, short hair, and they're smoking and drinking!

For a few years after WWI, Germans were really influenced by the cultural explosion in the USSR.

AVANT-GUARDE ART

IN THE U.S.S.R INFLUENCED GERMAN ART, LITERATURE, CINEMA, THEATRE AND MUSIC. ALL THESE NOW ENTERED A PERIOD OF GREAT CREATIVITY.

STREET THEATRE BROUGHT PLAYS TO THE PUBLIC, THE **CABARET** SCENE FLOURISHED AND **JAZZ BANDS** WERE POPULAR.

THERE WAS A CRAZE SURROUNDING BLACK AMERICAN DANCER **JOSEPHINE BAKER,** WHO APPEARED IN BERLIN'S *THEATER DES WESTENS* (THEATER OF THE WEST). SHE WAS DECLARED AN "EROTIC GODDESS" AND WAS ADMIRED BY MANY GERMANS.

I'm the first African-American woman who was accepted as beautiful in European terms.

Josephine Baker

It's surprising that Josephine Baker could be a superstar in Berlin, which would become the Nazi capital only a few years later.

ALL KINDS OF "ULTRAMODERN" FADS CAME AND WENT. ART AND A NEW TYPE OF ARCHITECTURE TAUGHT AT BAUHAUS ("ARCHITECTURE HOUSE") SCHOOLS REFLECTED THESE NEW IDEAS.

THERE WAS A DARING SPIRIT IN THE AIR, AND MANY ARTISTS AND INTELLECTUALS ENJOYED TEASING AND PROVOKING THE OLD-FASHIONED ESTABLISHMENT.

Artists like George Grosz were fined for defaming the military and for blasphemy.
I'm not at all impressed! Bourgeois intellectuals needed the establishment; they were psychologically tied to it like children to parents, and thought that by shocking it they were performing great revolutionary acts.

HITLER'S FIRST ATTEMPT

WHILE THE FRENCH AND BELGIANS WERE OCCUPYING THE RUHR IN 1923, ADOLF HITLER WAS MAKING POLITICAL SPEECHES IN MUNICH BRAUHAUSES, OR BEER HALLS.

He'd walk into a bar and start talking?
You bet. And he had thugs to protect him if anyone didn't want to have to listen to him.

THE NAZI PARTY'S MUSCLE WERE THE SO-CALLED **STORMTROOPERS** OR ***STURMABTEILUNG* (S.A).**

THESE MEN WORE BROWN SHIRTS AND THEY GUARDED HITLER AND HIS PARTY.

THE NAZI BROWNSHIRTS WOULD ROAM THE STREETS AND PICK FIGHTS WITH THE COMMUNIST *ROTKÄMPFERBUND* (RED FRONT FIGHTERS' LEAGUE), FOR WHOM THEY WERE MORE THAN A MATCH.

You take that, and that, and that, Commie bastards!

IN NOVEMBER 1923, HITLER AND SOME SUPPORTERS, INCLUDING A FEW WELL-KNOWN AND RESPECTABLE PEOPLE LIKE GENERAL LUDENDORFF, DECIDED TO TRY AND OVERTHROW EBERT'S GOVERNMENT.

HITLER'S PLAN WAS TO COPY WHAT ITALIAN FASCIST LEADER **BENITO MUSSOLINI** HAD DONE THE YEAR BEFORE, IN 1922, WHEN HE "MARCHED ON ROME" WITH HIS THUGS WHO WORE BLACK SHIRTS AND WERE CALLED *"SQUADRISTI"* (SQUAD MEMBERS). MUSSOLINI'S MEN HAD SO FRIGHTENED ITALIAN KING VICTOR EMANUEL III, THAT HE MADE MUSSOLINI PRIME MINISTER.

Marcia su Roma!

Benito Mussolini (on the left), marching to Rome in 1922.

HITLER WANTED TO TAKE ADVANTAGE OF A CONFLICT BETWEEN THE RIGHT-WING GOVERNMENT OF BAVARIA AND THE CENTRAL AUTHORITIES IN BERLIN. HE HOPED TO GET THE SUPPORT OF THE GENERAL PUBLIC FOR A **"MARCH ON BERLIN"** TO TOPPLE THE "TRAITOR GOVERNMENT OF SOCIALISTS AND JEWS".

ON THE EVENING OF NOVEMBER 8, 1923, HITLER BURST THEATRICALLY INTO MUNICH'S *BURGERBRAU* BEER HALL DRESSED IN HIS BEST COAT, HIS IRON CROSS PINNED TO A LAPEL, AND A STEEL HELMET ON HIS HEAD.

...HE THEN JUMPED UP ONTO A CHAIR AND FIRED INTO THE CEILING.

The National Revolution has broken out! No one may leave the hall. If you don't keep quiet I'll have a machine gun set up in the gallery, and use it.

...BUT THIS KIND OF REVOLUTION UNDER THE LEADERSHIP OF CORPORAL HITLER WASN'T WHAT LUDENDORFF AND THE MORE MAINSTREAM PARTICIPANTS IN THE *PUTSCH* WANTED. BESIDES, THE HEAD OF THE ARMY, GENERAL SEECKT, MADE IT CRYSTAL CLEAR TO THEM THAT THE ARMY WOULDN'T SUPPORT THEM.

A breach of the Constitution by individual adventurers, however patriotic their posture, *will not* be tolerated by the army.

General von Seeckt

EVENTUALLY, THE PEOPLE IN THE *BURGERBRAU* WERE ALLOWED TO LEAVE THE HALL, AND LUDENDORFF WALKED OUT WITH THEM.

...THAT WAS THE END OF HITLER'S CHANCE FOR A SUCCESSFUL COUP.

The *Burgerbrau* still exists; you can visit it and check out the bullet hole Hitler put in its ceiling.

THE NEXT DAY, NOVEMBER 9, 1923, HITLER SAW HIS ONLY CHANCE IN A PARADE THROUGH MUNICH AT THE HEAD OF HIS FOLLOWERS. HE HOPED THIS WAY TO GET THE PUBLIC TO JOIN HIM. BUT THINGS DIDN'T TURN OUT QUITE THE WAY HE WANTED. THE BAVARIAN POLICE FIRED ON HIS GROUP, AND FOURTEEN NAZIS AND FOUR POLICEMEN WERE KILLED.....

HITLER RAN AWAY.

TWO DAYS LATER, HE WAS FOUND HIDING IN THE ATTIC OF THE HOUSE OF ONE OF HIS WEALTHIER FOLLOWERS.

I was very depressed. .even considered suicide.

HE WAS ARRESTED AND TRIED FOR HIGH TREASON. THE PUNISHMENT FOR TRYING TO TAKE OVER THE GOVERNMENT BY FORCE WAS DEATH.

YET INSTEAD OF BEING EXECUTED, HITLER'S STAR NOW ROSE HIGH.

DURING HIS TRIAL HE BECAME A HOUSEHOLD NAME IN GERMANY.

I've found success of a sort in failure.

FOR THE FIRST TIME IN HIS POLITICAL CAREER, HITLER WAS ABLE TO EXPOUND HIS VIEWS TO THE BROAD PUBLIC.

MOST GERMAN NEWSPAPERS, BUT ALSO FOREIGN ONES, HAD REPORTS ON THE PASSIONATE, SELF-RIGHTEOUS AND PATRIOTIC TIRADES WITH WHICH HITLER JUSTIFIED HIMSELF IN COURT.

Rather than telling him to shut up, the judges let him go on and on about how he was only guilty of trying to help the country against the unfair demands of the Allies and Jews.

THE "IMPARTIAL" JUDGES WERE SO IMPRESSED THAT INSTEAD OF THE DEATH PENALTY THEY GAVE HITLER A FIVE-YEAR TERM IN PRISON.

Herr Hitler, I assure you as president of the court that you won't serve more than a fraction of the sentence.
PRESIDENT OF THE COURT

HITLER WAS SENT TO LANDSBERG PRISON IN BAVARIA.

A number of Nazi war criminals were hanged in this same prison in 1946.
I AM FROM TODAY

Adolf Hitler in his cell, wearing *lederhosen*
(traditional Bavarian shorts made of leather).

FOR GOOD BEHAVIOR, HE SERVED ONLY NINE MONTHS.
Good behavior?
IN PRISON, HITLER RECEIVED A STEADY STREAM OF FAN MAIL.
Yeah, all he did was dictate his racist autobiography to his associate, Rudolf Hess.

ADOLF HITLER
MEIN KAMPF

THE BOOK'S ORIGINAL TITLE WAS *FOUR-AND-A-HALF YEARS OF STRUGGLE AGAINST LIES, STUPIDITY AND COWARDICE.*

HIS NAZI PUBLISHER KNEW BETTER AND SHORTENED IT TO *MEIN KAMPF,* SIMPLY "MY STRUGGLE" OR "MY BATTLE".

...BUT MORE ON THIS LATER.

WHEN HIS TERM ENDED AND HITLER WALKED OUT OF LANDSBERG PRISON IN 1925, HE ANNOUNCED THAT HIS NAZI PARTY WOULD RENOUNCE VIOLENCE AND PROMISED THAT THE N.S.D.A.P WOULD ONLY ATTEMPT TO COME TO POWER BY LEGAL MEANS.

I forsake violence.

Don't believe him! He's just saying that because his SA brownshirts have temporarily been made illegal by the government!

HITLER SAW THAT WHILE HE WAS IN PRISON, SUPPORT FOR HIS EXTREMIST PARTY HAD DECREASED. THIS WAS BECAUSE THE ECONOMY HAD IMPROVED AND THERE WERE NOW FEWER ANGRY PEOPLE WILLING TO LISTEN TO THE NAZI MESSAGE OF HATE.

Whatever you say about Hitler, he was politically flexible and able to learn what approach was the most fruitful.

TEMPORARY STABILITY

DURING THE 1923 RUHR CRISIS, THE ISOLATIONIST AMERICANS HAD CLEARLY SEEN THE DANGER OF GERMANY DESCENDING INTO ANARCHY AND CHAOS. THAT COULD LEAD TO COMMUNISM.

We definitely don't want communism in Germany!

THERE WAS ANOTHER PROBLEM, TOO. WHEN THE GERMANS WERE SLOW TO PAY REPARATIONS TO FRANCE AND BRITAIN, THE GOVERNMENTS IN PARIS AND LONDON TOLD WASHINGTON THEY WERE UNABLE TO REPAY THEIR WAR LOANS TO AMERICA.

These damn American war loans! The whole world owes money to the American banks!

SO IN NOVEMBER 1923 THE U.S.A. AND BRITAIN AGREED TO WORK TOGETHER WITH FRANCE TO DEAL WITH THE GERMAN REPARATIONS QUESTION. A TEAM WAS FORMED UNDER AMERICAN FINANCIER **CHARLES DAWES** TO FIND A SOLUTION TO THE PROBLEM.

Phew, what a relief!

THE FRENCH WERE VERY HAPPY BECAUSE - FINALLY - THEY WEREN'T ALONE IN TRYING TO GET THE GERMANS TO PAY THE REPARATIONS SET BY THE TREATY OF VERSAILLES.

Charles Dawes

IN 1924, MISTER DAWES CAME UP WITH A FIVE-YEAR PLAN FOR GERMAN REPARATIONS PAYMENTS. THESE WERE TO BE GUARANTEED BY GERMAN ASSETS, SUCH AS RAILWAYS, SOME PROFITABLE INDUSTRIES, AND ALSO BY CERTAIN TAXES.

What does "guaranteed" mean?
Simple. If the Germans don't pay, we just take those things from them.
THE **DAWES PLAN** DIDN'T DETERMINE THE TOTAL AMOUNT GERMANY WOULD NOW OWE. NEITHER DID IT FIX A DATE FOR THE END OF REPARATIONS. HOWEVER, IT DID SIGNIFICANTLY REDUCE THE PAYMENTS THAT GERMANY WOULD HAVE TO MAKE UNTIL 1929, WHEN THE SITUATION WAS TO BE REEVALUATED.

THE FIVE YEARS OF THE DAWES PLAN, 1924-29, WERE THE "GOLDEN AGE" OF REPARATIONS. THE ALLIES, ESPECIALLY FRANCE, RECEIVED PAYMENTS IN CASH AND KIND WITH GREATER REGULARITY THAN EVER.

We French accept the Dawes Plan. Most of our post-war reconstruction has been completed anyway. Now at least our wartime allies, Britain and the US, are helping us get reparations from the Germans.
We Germans pay, but we protest! When will the Allies stop milking us dry?!

...dry? You're exaggerating! Germany has always had the capacity to pay reparations to the full. Only it never wanted to as it never repented for its awful crimes in WWI!

With American money coming in...
...everyone must calm down!

BYT THE DAWES PLAN HAD A SMALL PROBLEM: IT DIDN'T LINK GERMAN PAYMENTS AND ALLIED REPAYMENT OF WAR DEBTS TO THE UNITED STATES. YES, THE AMERICAN PLAN MADE IT EASIER FOR THE GERMANS TO PAY REPARATIONS, BUT THERE WAS ALWAYS THE CHANCE THAT IF IN THE FUTURE THEY DIDN'T PAY, NEITHER WOULD THE FRENCH, BRITISH, AND OTHER DEBTORS REPAY THEIR WAR LOANS TO THE U.S.A.

FOR THE TIME BEING THOUGH, EVERYTHING SEEMED TO BE GOING WELL IN GERMANY.

GUSTAV STRESEMANN WAS CHANCELLOR FOR THREE MONTHS. HE THEN BECAME FOREIGN MINISTER, AND CONTINUED TO LEAD GERMANY FROM THAT POSITION.

Gustav Stresemann

UNDER STRESEMANN, THE COUNTRY SEEMED TO BE ENTERING A PERIOD OF STABILITY. THE *REICHSMARK* WAS REPLACED BY THE *RENTENMARK* AND THE CURRENCY WAS STABILIZED.

CONSERVATIVES IN GERMANY LIKED STRESEMANN, SO THERE WAS LESS PRESSURE ON HIS GOVERNMENT.

STRESEMANN HAD BEGUN HIS POLITICAL CAREER AS A NATIONALIST. ALTHOUGH HE'D INITIALLY SYMPATHIZED WITH THE KAPP *PUTSCH* IN 1920, HE HATED POLITICAL VIOLENCE AND INSTABILITY. AND SO BECAME A DEMOCRAT.

STRESEMANN WAS VERY IMPORTANT FOR GERMAN STABILITY. IN FACT, HE WAS ONE OF THREE MAIN REASONS THE WEIMAR REPUBLIC LASTED AS LONG AS IT DID - 14 YEARS, FROM 1919 TO 1933.

THE SECOND REASON WAS **FIELD MARSHAL PAUL VON HINDENBURG**, *JUNKER*, HERO OF THE BATTLE OF TANNENBERG IN EAST PRUSSIA (WHEN THE GERMANS BEAT THE RUSSIANS AT THE START OF WORLD WAR ONE), AND HEAD OF GERMANY'S ARMY FOR MOST OF THE WAR.

I'm a true German patriot!

ON FEBRUARY 28, 1925, PRESIDENT EBERT DIED AFTER HAVING POSTPONED AN APPENDICITIS OPERATION FOR TOO LONG IN ORDER TO FIGHT A LIBEL SUIT AGAINST THE EDITOR OF A NATIONALIST NEWSPAPER THAT HAD CALLED HIM A TRAITOR.

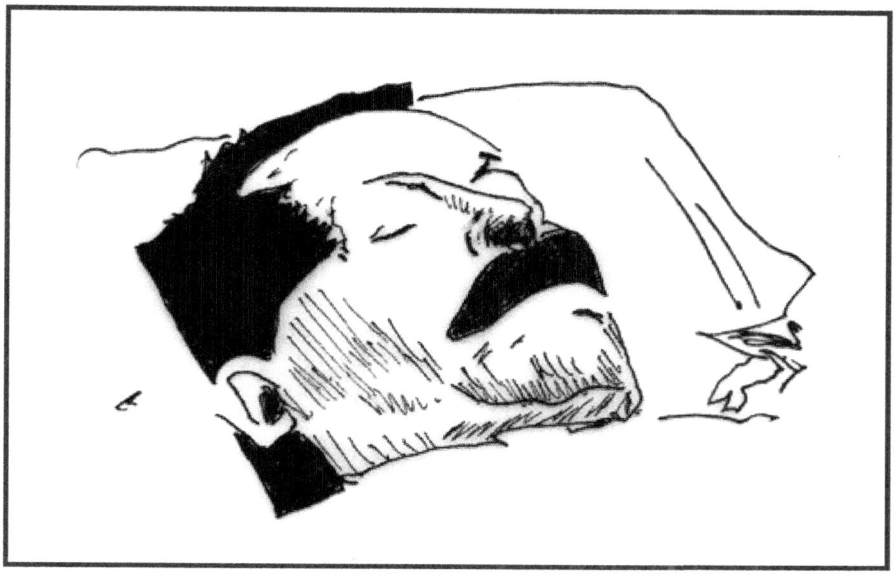

Geez, these nationalists are a pain!
What's a libel suit?
?
That's when people take you to court for saying bad things about them that aren't true.
LAW

IN THE ELECTIONS FOR A NEW PRESIDENT IN 1925, HINDENBURG WON BY A SMALL MARGIN. HE RECEIVED 14,600,000 VOTES AGAINST 13,700,000 FOR WILHELM MARX, CANDIDATE FOR A COALITION OF SOCIAL DEMOCRATS AND THE CATHOLIC CENTER PARTY.

Because the Communists and Social Democrats refused to join any coalition together, Hindenburg's victory wasn't unexpected.

ANOTHER IMPORTANT REASON FOR THE LACK OF COOPERATION BETWEEN THE COMMUNISTS AND SOCIAL DEMOCRATS WAS THAT THE SOVIET UNION INSISTED SOCIAL DEMOCRATS WERE "TRAITORS" OF THE WORKING CLASS, AND EVEN CALLED THEM "SOCIAL FASCISTS", OR PEOPLE WHO DIFFERED VERY LITTLE FROM THE REAL FASCISTS.

We Communists remember the SPD's role against us in 1919!
GERMAN COMMUNIST

The Germans want no president in a top hat. He must wear a uniform and plenty of decorations.

Gustav Stressemann

HINDENBURG'S ELECTION WAS AN EXPRESSION OF NOSTALGIA FOR THE "OLD GERMANY" OF THE *KAISER* AND THE *JUNKERS*.

THE SAME FORCES THAT HAD RULED THE *REICH* OF THE *KAISER* HAD ONCE MORE GAINED THE UPPER HAND IN GERMANY.
YET THERE WAS ONE VERY POSITIVE THING ABOUT HINDENBURG. THOUGH VERY CONSERVATIVE HIMSELF, HE WAS ABLE TO KEEP THE EXTREME RIGHT WING UNDER CHECK. THIS TASK WAS MADE EASIER BY THE RELATIVELY GOOD TIMES THAT FOLLOWED THE DAWES PLAN. THERE WERE FEWER ANGRY PEOPLE WILLING TO LISTEN TO LUNATIC FRINGE RIGHT-WINGERS LIKE THE NAZIS.
How long will things be okay economically?
Wait and see what happens in 1929!
THE THIRD REASON THE WEIMAR REPUBLIC LASTED FOURTEEN YEARS WAS THE ALLIES, WHO DIDN'T WANT TO SEE GERMANY SINK INTO ANARCHY AND PERHAPS BECOME COMMUNIST. THIS MEANT THEY WEREN'T GOING TO LET THE COUNTRY BECOME POOR.

CHANCELLOR STRESEMANN'S LONG-TERM AIM WAS TO REMOVE THE ALLIED TROOPS THAT THE TREATY OF VERSAILLES HAD STATIONED IN RHINELAND CITIES. HE DIDN'T KNOW HOW TO DO THIS...UNTIL ONE DAY HE HAD AN IDEA.

I have a bold proposal!

Stressemann

Locarno, Switzerland

IN LOCARNO, IN FEBRUARY 1925, STRESEMANN PROPOSED A VOLUNTARY GERMAN GUARANTEE OF ITS WESTERN BORDERS. HE SAID THAT GERMANY NO LONGER WANTED ALSACE AND LORRAINE FROM FRANCE, OR EUPEN AND MALMEDY FROM BELGIUM.

EVERYONE THOUGHT THIS WAS A GREAT SIGN. THE GERMANS THEMSELVES WERE NOW ACCEPTING WHAT VERSAILLES HAD SAID WERE THE COUNTRY'S WESTERN BORDERS!
THE ONLY PEOPLE WHO WEREN'T EXCITED WERE GERMANY'S NEIGHBORS TO THE EAST - THE **POLES** AND THE **CZECHS**.
About our eastern borders set by the Treaty of Versailles...are these under question now?
Tak?
POLE
CZECH

THE **LOCARNO PACT** WAS SIGNED BY GERMANY, FRANCE, BRITAIN, ITALY, AND BELGIUM, ON OCTOBER 16, 1925.

WHAT DID THE GERMANS GAIN BY THE LOCARNO PACT?

WELL, THEY NOW CAME ACROSS AS WELL-BEHAVED AND COOPERATIVE.

MORE IMPORTANTLY, FRANCE COULD NO LONGER LEGALLY INVADE GERMANY, OR HAVE HOPES OF AN INDEPENDENT RHINELAND STATE EVER BEING CREATED.

We like the sound of that, too!

MANY PEOPLE THOUGHT THE LOCARNO AGREEMENT A WONDERFUL SIGN THAT EUROPE WAS FINALLY ON THE ROAD TO PEACE AND STABILITY.

BUT THE FEW PEOPLE WHO LOOKED DEEPER INTO PROBLEMS (AND THEY'RE ALWAYS THE MINORITY), WEREN'T SO OPTIMISTIC....

THE **LOCARNO AGREEMENT** WAS ODD BECAUSE IN A STRANGE WAY IT REPLACED THE EXISTING LAW (THE TREATY OF VERSAILLES) WITH A PROMISE BY THE GERMANS TO RESPECT THE BORDERS IT HAD SET.

...THE PESSIMISTS WERE WORRIED WITH GOOD REASON. WHO COULD SAY IN 1925 WHAT WOULD HAPPEN IF A FUTURE GOVERNMENT IN GERMANY SIMPLY REFUSED TO ACCEPT THE COUNTRY'S WESTERN BORDERS?

Germany at Locarno was like a school bully telling every-one he's going to be good, instead of the teachers and kids telling him that he *has* to be good.
And the Locarno Pact didn't commit Germany to accept the territorial settlement in the east.

THE LOCARNO PACT SAID NOTHING ABOUT GERMANY ACCEPTING HER EASTERN FRONTIER WITH POLAND AND CZECHOSLOVAKIA AS UNALTERABLE. ALL STRESEMANN WOULD SAY ON THAT SCORE WAS THAT ANY CHANGE MUST COME ABOUT PEACEFULLY.

Things wouldn't happen that way.
OWL OF WISDOM

THE LOCARNO PACT MERELY RECOGNIZED FRANCE'S PROMISES TO POLAND AND CZECHOSLOVAKIA.

WHAT WERE THESE COMMITMENTS? FRANCE HAD SIGNED AGREEMENTS WITH POLAND IN 1921 AND CZECHOSLOVAKIA IN 1924. SHE'D DONE THIS BECAUSE AT A TIME WHEN THE UNITED STATES OF AMERICA HAD WITHDRAWN FROM EUROPE AND BRITAIN WAS REVERTING TO HER TRADITIONAL ISOLATION, FRANCE HOPED TO FORCE GERMANY INTO HAVING TO FIGHT ON TWO FRONTS IF WAR EVER BROKE OUT AGAIN.

How's France going to keep these diplomatic commitments without violating Germany's western frontiers?
Take a look at a map! How's France going to reach us Czechs and Poles if we need help against Germany?

Polish Minister of Defense Joseph Pilsudski

Czech statesman Edvard Benes

FRANCE ACCEPTED THE LOCARNO PACT BECAUSE SHE'D FINALLY THROWN IN THE TOWEL ON TRYING TO CONTROL GERMANY. THE RUHR CRISIS HAD TAUGHT HER THIS IMPORTANT LESSON.

SO FRANCE CHANGED STRATEGY AND NOW TRIED TO DRAW GERMANY INTO INTERNATIONAL AGREEMENTS GUARANTEED BY OTHER POWERS.

OTHER REWARDS GERMANY RECEIVED FOR GOOD BEHAVIOR INCLUDED THE JANUARY 1926 WITHDRAWAL OF BRITISH FORCES FROM RHINELAND CITIES. THE NEXT YEAR, 1927, THE INTER-ALLIED CONTROL COMMISSION ALSO PACKED ITS BAGS AND LEFT GERMANY.

Yes, and the French withdrew in August of 1929.

BY PROPOSING AND SIGNING THE TREATY, STRESEMANN PAVED THE WAY FOR THE ACCEPTANCE OF GERMANY, "IN THE SPIRIT OF LOCARNO", INTO THE **LEAGUE OF NATIONS** IN 1926.

I believe the Locarno Treaty will bring diplomatic stability to Europe.

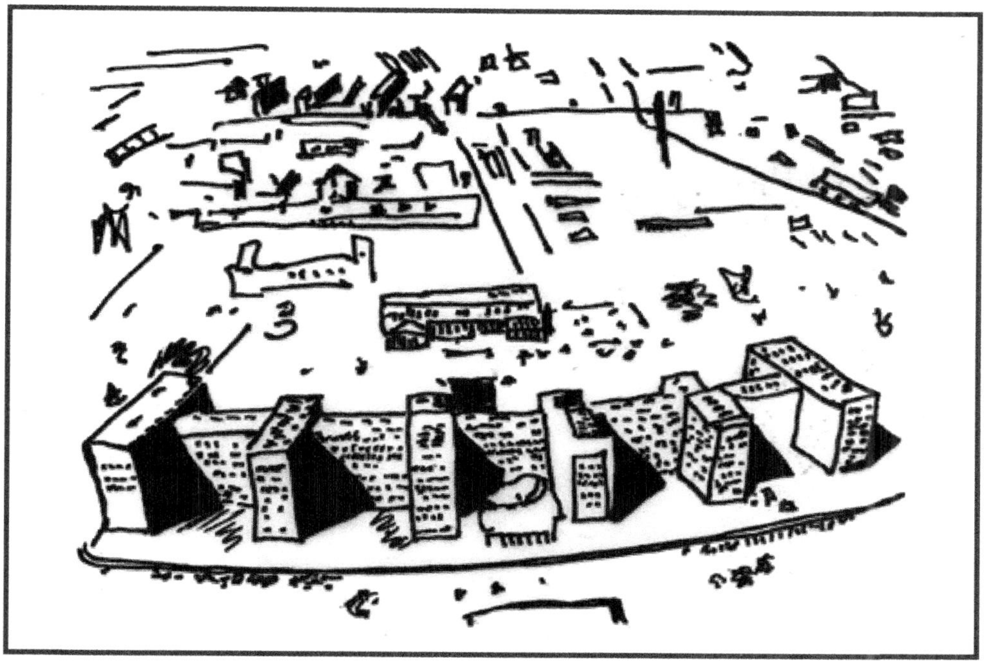

IN THE LATE 1920s IT LOOKED FROM THE OUTSIDE THAT GERMANY WAS THE PICTURE OF WELL-BEING AND STABILITY.

GIANT INDUSTRIAL COMPANIES APPEARED IN 1926, COMPANIES LIKE THE **I.G. FARBEN** CHEMICAL INDUSTY CONGLOMERATE, AND **UNITED STEELWORKS** (***VEREINIGTE STAHLWERKE***).

IN 1927 THE ECONOMY'S OVERALL PRODUCTION FIGURES AT LAST MATCHED THOSE OF 1913.

IN 1928 THE OPTIMISTIC, PEACE-LOVING SPIRIIT OF LOCARNO LED THE LEADERS OF MANY COUNTRIES TO SIGN THE ANTI-WAR **KELLOGG-BRIAND PACT.**

Kellogg?
As in Kellogg's
cornflakes?

No, he wasn't from
that American family.

Frank Kellogg

Aristide Briand

FRANK KELLOGG WAS AMERICAN SECRETARY OF STATE (AS THE AMERICANS CALL THEIR FOREIGN MINISTER). **ARISTIDE BRIAND** WAS FRENCH FOREIGN MINISTER. THE DOCUMENT THEY DREW UP MADE WAR ILLEGAL.

Ha! Ha!

THE KELLOGG-BRIAND PACT REPRESENTED OPTIMISM FOR PEACE IN THE FUTURE. IT WAS SIGNED BY 54 COUNTRIES, INCLUDING SOVIET RUSSIA. BUT THE PACT HAD A SERIOUS WEAK SPOT: THERE WAS NO PUNISHMENT FOR COUNTRIES THAT DIDN'T RESPECT IT AND BEGAN WARS.

Still, it was an important commitment to peace by many countries.
POLITICALLY CORRECT
So? What was the Kellogg-Briand Pact going to do if nations violated it?

Locarno and German membership in the League of Nations have brought political stability to Europe!
OPTIMIST

...IT SEEMED TO OPTIMISTS THAT THE POLICY OF RECONCILIATION WAS GOING WELL. AS WE'VE SEEN (A FEW TIMES ALREADY), THE AMERICAN MONEY OF THE DAWES PLAN MADE IT POSSIBLE FOR GERMANY TO KEEP ON PAYING REPARATIONS ON A REGULAR BASIS.

THE SIGNS WERE GOOD FOR THE WEIMAR REPUBLIC. THE PARLIAMENTARY ELECTIONS IN MAY 1928 GAVE THE WORST RESULT IN A DECADE FOR ITS SWORN ENEMIES. TOGETHER, THE NATIONALISTS, NAZIS, AND COMMUNISTS WERE UNABLE TO GET MORE THAN 30 PERCENT OF THE VOTE.

UNDER THE YOUNG PLAN, THE UNITED STATES LENT MONEY TO GERMANY SO GERMANY COULD PAY REDEMPTION TO FRANCE, SO FRANCE COULD PAY BACK ITS WAR LOANS TO THE UNITED STATES.

HERE'S A DIAGRAM THAT MIGHT MAKE THIS SCHEME MORE UNDERSTANDABLE.

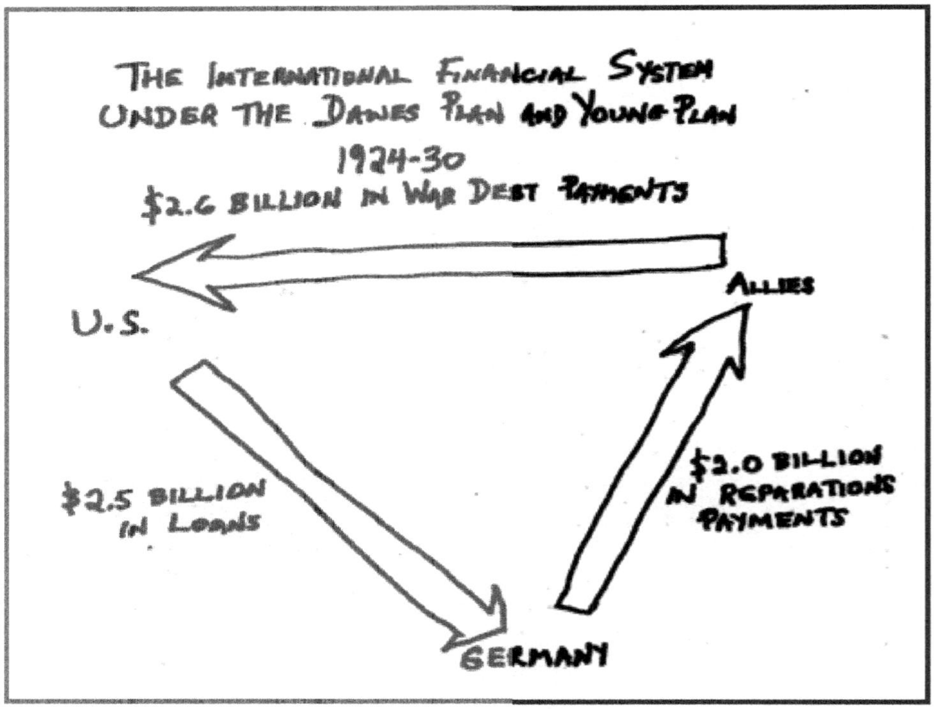

THE YOUNG PLAN REDUCED THE SUM GERMANY HAD TO PAY BY 70 PERCENT - TO 121 BILLION *REICHSMARKS*. IT LINKED FRENCH AND BRITISH DEBTS TO GERMAN PAYMENTS...WHICH SOUNDS CONFUSING BUT SIMPLY MEANS THAT THE FRENCH AND BRITISH WOULD PAY BACK AMERICAN BANKS FOR THEIR WORLD WAR ONE LOANS ONLY AFTER THE GERMANS PAID THEM REPARATIONS.

THE YOUNG PLAN SET **1988** AS THE **FINAL YEAR** OF PAYMENTS.

Weren't German reparations finally paid in 2010?
Yes, repayment was interrupted by Hitler, which delayed the final pay-off to 1996 However, a clause added to the agreement after WWII said that Germany would have to pay interest on the bill if she were ever to reunite, which she did in 1990. So the final historic payment of 59 million British pouncs was made on Sunday, October 3, 2010, ninety-two years after WWI ended.

THE YOUNG PLAN MEANT AMERICA CONTINUED TO BE SERIOUSLY INVOLVED IN EUROPEAN POLITICS.

BUT SOMETHING WAS VERY WRONG UNDER BOTH THE DAWES AND THE YOUNG PLAN. GERMANY DEPENDED ON HUGE FOREIGN INVESTMENTS, TWO THIRDS OF WHICH WERE OF COURSE AMERICAN.

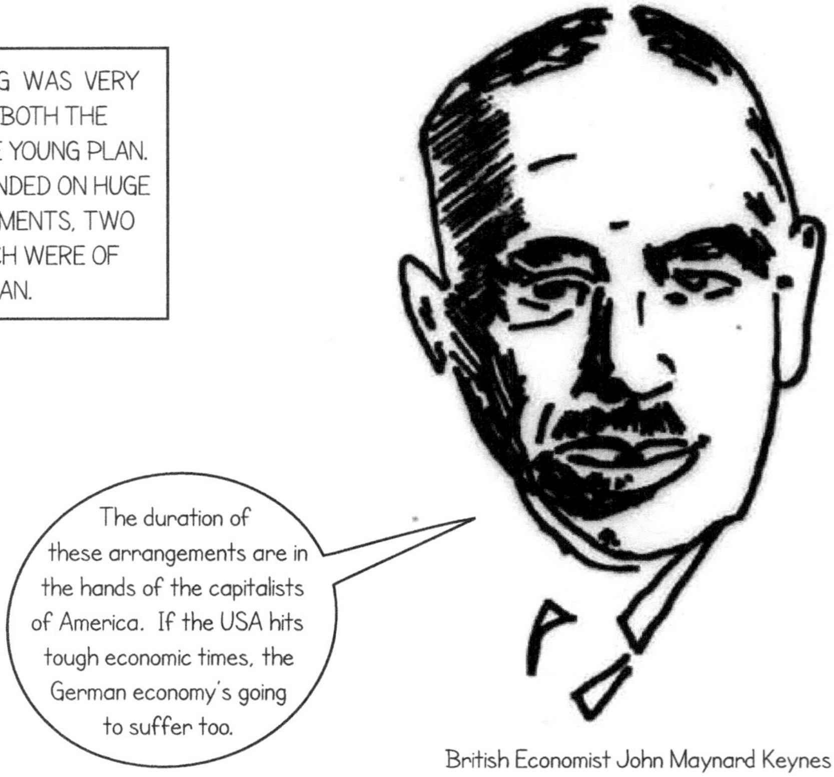
The duration of these arrangements are in the hands of the capitalists of America. If the USA hits tough economic times, the German economy's going to suffer too.

British Economist John Maynard Keynes

SO....WHILE EVERYTHING SEEMED ALRIGHT ON THE SURFACE, THINGS WEREN'T SO GOOD BENEATH IT.

THE BASIS OF THE GERMAN ECONOMY WAS FLAWED. GERMANY DEPENDED WAY TOO MUCH ON INTERNATIONAL INVESTMENTS.
It's 1928 and Germany's dancing on a volcano!
The country also buys more goods than it sells and has a deficit of 500 million marks!
Gustav Stresemann
This ain't good, it ain't at all good, I say.
MORE THAN TWO-THIRDS OF ALL CAPITAL INVESTED IN GERMANY IN THE LATE 1920s CAME FROM FOREIGN LOANS.

PUT SIMPLY, GERMANY WAS DEPENDENT ON THINGS GOING WELL IN THE ECONOMIES OF THE COUNTRIES THAT INVESTED IN HER. FIRST AND FOREMOST, THAT WAS THE UNITED STATES OF AMERICA.

THEN SUDDENLY... THE SITUATION BEGAN TO GET WORSE, FAST. FIRST, STRESEMANN DIED OF A HEART ATTACK, ON OCTOBER 3, 1929.

HE WAS ONLY 51.

THREE WEEKS LATER, ON **OCTOBER 24, 1929,** AS THE VALUE OF SHARES FELL SHARPLY, THE

WALL STREET STOCK MARKET IN NEW YORK **CRASHED**

WALL ST.

It was a lot like 2008. Banks lent too much money to people who couldn't pay, and the bubble burst.
SOUNDS FAMILIAR

THE WALL STREET CRASH WAS THE STORY OF BANKS LENDING EASY MONEY IN AN ATMOSPHERE OF UNLIMITED ENTHUSIASM FOR THE PLEASURES AND TOYS OF A MODERN CONSUMER SOCIETY.

Drink
Coca-Cola

THE WALL STREET CRASH, WHICH WAS THE TRIGGER OF THE GREAT DEPRESSION - THE HUGE ECONOMIC SLUMP THAT LASTED TEN YEARS AND LED TO WORLD WAR TWO - ALSO HAD A LOT TO DO WITH AMERICAN BANKS LENDING MONEY TO OTHER COUNTRIES *BEFORE* COLLECTING THE WAR LOANS. THIS WAY, AMERICAN BANKERS GOT THEMSELVES, AND THE REST OF THE WORLD, INTO A HUGE FINANCIAL HOLE.

It was all the US bankers' fault! They shouldn't have lent anything to anyone during the war!

THE VIEW THAT THE U.S.A SHOULDN 'T HAVE EVEN JOINED WORLD WAR ONE DID EXIST AT THE TIME, BUT IT DIDN'T TAKE THE REALITY OF THE WAR INTO ACCOUNT. AMERICAN ISOLATIONISM WASN'T A REALISTIC POLICY BECAUSE THE RISK WAS THAT A VICTORIOUS GERMANY WOULD TREATEN AMERICA'S NEWLY GAINED SUPERPOWER STATUS.

We became a superpower for the first time in 1914, when we completed construction of the Panama Canal. This gave us huge advantages for world trade.

PANAMA CANAL

WHEN THE BOTTOM FELL OUT OF NEW YORK'S FINANCIAL MARKET IN OCTOBER 1929. AMERICAN BANKERS CALLED THEIR LOANS, DEMANDING THE IMMEDIATE RETURN OF ALL OF THEIR MONEY.

IN A SHORT PERIOD OF TIME, THE CRISIS WAS TRANSFORMED FROM AN ECONOMIC TO A GENERAL ONE, AND FROM A NORTH AMERICAN CRISIS TO A GLOBAL CRISIS.

THE DEEPER CAUSES OF THE CRISIS (BEYOND THE ACTIONS OF GREEDY BANKERS) WAS THE GENERAL OVERPRODUCTION OF GOODS. CAPITALIST ECONOMIES MEAN COMPETITION FOR PROFITS AMONG MANY DIFFERENT PRODUCERS, WHICH MAKES PLANNING THE NUMBER OF COMMODITIES TO PUT ON THE MARKET IMPOSSIBLE.

SINCE A LOT FEWER PEOPLE WERE ABLE TO BUY THE PRODUCTS THAT INDUSTRY PRODUCED, PROFITS FELL EVERYWHERE. TO RESTORE PROFITABILITY, PRODUCERS CUT COSTS BY SACKING WORKERS AND LOWERING THEIR WAGES.

MANY COMPANIES WENT BANKRUPT AND THERE WAS A LARGE-SCALE WITHDRAWAL OF CAPITAL FROM ALL MARKETS, INCLUDING GERMANY'S.

BANK OF THE U. S. A
The Americans could've saved the world from the Great Depression if they'd forgiven the war loans the English, French, Germans and others had taken out. Hell, they made enough money out of the war anyway!
Ha! Forgive the loans!

THE FOREIGN CAPITAL (AGAIN, MOSTLY AMERICAN MONEY) INVESTED IN GERMANY'S COMPANIES, CITIES AND STATES, WAS 5 BILLION MARKS IN 1928. THIS FIGURE DROPPED BY HALF IN 1929, AND WAS JUST 700 MILLION IN 1930!

THIS WAS THE END OF THE SPIRIT OF INTERNATIONAL COOPERATION. IN SHORT, WORLD TRADE WAS DEAD.

Now it's everyone for themselves!

BANKER
We'll print money and raise protective tariff barriers so our production isn't hurt by cheaper foreign goods. This'll minimize the domestic effects of the crisis.

COUNTRY AFTER COUNTRY ABANDONED THE GOLD STANDARD. IN OTHER WORDS, CENTRAL BANKS (THE MOST IMPORTANT AND STATE-CONTROLLED BANK OF EACH COUNTRY) DIDN'T LIMIT THE AMOUNT OF CASH THEY PRINTED TO THE AMOUNT OF GOLD HELD BY THE STATE...

THE EFFECT OF THE GREAT DEPRESSION ON INTERNATIONAL POLITICS WAS FOR COUNTRIES TO TURN INWARD. THEY ALL FOCUSED ON DOMESTIC PROBLEMS, AND TRIED TO BALANCE THEIR BUDGETS.
THE GREAT DEPRESSION MADE IT SEEM OBVIOUS AT A TIME OF GENERAL BELT-TIGHTENING THAT SPENDING LOTS OF MONEY ON WEAPONS WASN'T A BRIGHT IDEA.
See, there *is* a bright side to the Great Depression! Nations aren't spending so much on their militaries anymore.
Another war would be insanity!
In these circumstances, the expense of another war's unthinkable.
BECAUSE OF THE MASSIVE WITHDRAWAL OF AMERICAN MONEY FROM GERMANY, THE GERMAN GOVERNMENT APPROACHED PRESIDENT HERBERT HOOVER IN OCTOBER OF 1930, AND ASKED FOR A SUSPENSION (OR MORATORIUM) OF REPARATION PAYMENTS.
HOOVER HAD NO CHOICE BUT TO AGREE...

My moratorium freezes all debts between countries from mid-1930 to mid-1932.
US President Herbert Hoover
BY THE END OF 1931, IT WAS CLEAR THAT THE DEPRESSION WOULD LAST MUCH LONGER.
IN DECEMBER 1931, IN BASLE, SWITZERLAND, COUNTRIES INVOLVED WITH THE YOUNG PLAN AGREED TO CHANGE ALL DEBTS BETWEEN GOVERNMENTS.

THE NEXT STEP WAS THE LAUSANNE CONFERENCE OF JUNE 1932, WHICH AGREED THAT GERMAN REPARATIONS MUST BE ENDED BY A LUMP SUM PAYMENT OF 3,000 MILLION MARKS.
I AM PROTESTING
Wait just one minute, please! That's forgiving the Germans 90 percent of their outstanding debt!
Angry Frenchman

THE U.S. GOVERNMENT WAS VERY ANGRY WHEN THE EUROPEAN COUNTRIES INSISTED THAT THEIR WAR-DEBT REPAYMENTS SHOULD ALSO BE TERMINATED! BUT THERE WAS NOTHING THAT WASHINGTON COULD DO ABOUT IT...

And just like that, the financial agreements of Versailles ceased to exist.

RISE OF THE RIGHT

Arbeit!

WITH THE WORLD'S ECONOMY IN THE DUMPS, POPULAR ANTI-DEMOCRATIC MOVEMENTS ROSE UP IN MANY COUNTRIES. PEOPLE BEGAN TO LISTEN TO EXTREME SOLUTIONS, LIKE BOLSHEVISM OR FASCISM.

WE MUSTN'T FORGET THAT DESPITE GERMAN NAZISM'S PARTICULAR INTENSITY, OTHER COUNTRIES, LIKE FRANCE, SPAIN, BELGIUM, AND BRITAIN, WEREN'T IMMUNE FROM THE FORCES THAT HAD MADE HITLER AND NAZISM POSSIBLE IN GERMANY.

UNEMPLOYMENT IN GERMANY WAS MASSIVE. IF IN THE MIDDLE OF 1929, 1.5 MILLION PEOPLE WERE JOBLESS, THE NUMBER WAS 3 MILLION IN 1930, AND 6 MILLION ONE YEAR LATER, IN 1931!

IF THE PARTY OF "POWER", THE **SOCIAL DEMOCRATS (S.P.D)**, HAD THE HIGHEST SUPPORT IN 1928, IT WAS ALL DOWN HILL ONCE THE GREAT DEPRESSION HIT.

We can help the poor with our extreme solutions!

KPD leader Ernst Thälmann

HELP
IN THE CRISIS, THE COMMUNISTS GOT GREATER SUPPORT THAN EVER. ABOVE ALL, THOUGH, IT WAS THE NAZIS WHO GAINED FROM ECONOMIC HARD TIMES.

It's much more difficult, intellectually at least, to be a Communist. My theories and those of Engels, Lenin, Trotsky, *et al*, are much more complex than the simple-minded books on hatred that the extreme right produces.

Karl Marx

Why didn't the Communists attract more people than the Nazis?
NEVERTHELESS, THE RISE TO POWER OF HITLER AND HIS NAZI PARTY WAS NOT A FOREGONE CONCLUSION, EVEN AS LATE AS 1932. THE GROWTH IN MEMBERSHIP OF THE K.P.D DUE TO MASS UNEMPLOYMENT MEANT THAT HITLER AND THE NAZIS FACED REAL COMPETITION FROM THE LEFT.

THE ORGANIZATIONAL AND PROPAGANDISTIC INNOVATIONS OF THE NAZI PARTY, ESPECIALLY THE N.S.D.A.P's ABILITY TO APPEAL TO VERY DIFFERENT GROUPS IN SOCIETY, DID IN THE END LEAD TO HITLER TAKING POWER ON JANUARY 30, 1933.

A HISTORIAN MUST ALWAYS STRIVE TO BE OBJECTIVE. WE MAY HATE HITLER AND EVERYTHING HE STOOD FOR, BUT IT WOULDN'T BE HONEST NOT TO ADMIT THAT HIS SHEER FORCE OF WILL, CHARISMATIC PERSONALITY, AND POLITICAL GENIUS WERE A VERY UNIQUE AND POWERFUL BLEND OF LEADERSHIP CHARACTERISTICS.

It was an unfortunate coincidence of history that at that time in Germany there was a demagogue with the powerful personality and political ability of Hitler.

Men make their own history, but they do not make it as they please; they do not make it under self-selected circumstances, but under circumstances existing already, given and transmitted from the past.

Karl means that without the situation in Germany at the time, Adolf Hitler would have remained an unknown.

WE'LL SEE THAT TIME AFTER TIME (AT LEAST BEFORE THE SECOND WORLD WAR BEGAN IN 1939), HITLER PROVIDED THE NECESSARY LEADERSHIP THAT SAVED THE NAZI PARTY FROM DESTRUCTION. HE ALSO HAD AN UNCANNY TALENT FOR POLITICAL PATIENCE AND FOR KNOWING THE RIGHT TIME TO ACT.
HITLER WAS SUCH A TALENTED ORATOR, HE WAS THE MAIN MAGNET IN THE NAZI PARTY.
He used a variety of "tricks" of public speaking, like sarcasm and appeal to emotion, but those weren't the only ways he attracted listeners.
WHEN HITLER SPOKE, MANY GERMANS WERE DRAWN TO HIM BECAUSE HE CAME ACROSS AS INTENSELY **PATRIOTIC** AND MADE THEM FEEL THAT HE TRULY RELATED TO THEIR ANGER AND FRUSTRATION.
AS A PERSON, HITLER WAS LAZY BUT HE HAD A KILLER POLITICAL INSTINCT, WAS EXTREMELY SELF-CONFIDENT, AND HAD AN ABILITY TO GET PEOPLE FROM ALL WALKS OF LIFE TO BE FANATICALLY DEVOTED TO HIM.
People in Germany wanted a miracle man!

HITLER PRESENTED HIMSELF AS A SIMPLE FRONT-LINE SOLDIER WHO'D RETURNED TO THE FATHERLAND TO BE **THE MESSIAH** OF THE GERMAN PEOPLE.

I'll make the heads of the November criminals roll!

HE WAS EVEN GREATER A SHOWMAN THAN *KAISER* WILHELM II HAD BEEN.

ALBERT **SPEER**, AN ARCHITECT WHO LATER BECAME HITLER'S MINISTER OF ARMAMENTS AND MANUFACTURING, WAS THE MAN WHO KNEW HIM BEST. HE SAID THAT, MORE THAN ANYTHING ELSE, ADOLPH HITLER WAS AN ACTOR - A *SCHAUSPIELER*.

HE USED SIMPLE, STRAIGHTFORWARD LANGUAGE THAT ORDINARY PEOPLE COULD UNDERSTAND, SHORT SENTENCES AND POWERFUL, EMOTIONAL SLOGANS.
A Hitler speech was a show that was full of a kind of revivalist fervor, intensity, and fanaticism.
There were no qualifications in what he said. Everything was absolute and final, black and white.

IT WAS IMPOSSIBLE FOR LESS DEMAGOGIC POLITICIANS TO MATCH THE POWERFUL MAGNETISM OF HITLER'S SPEECHES.
How can an honest person who bases his or her arguments on logic compete with someone who's willing to twist the truth in order to present the best possible picture to the naïve listener?
It was like Hitler was a tricky adult talking to naïve children.

IN THE COURSE OF HIS CAREER, HITLER DISPLAYED AN UNUSUAL CAPACITY FOR INGRATIATING HIMSELF WITH PEOPLE WHO WERE ORIGINALLY SUSPICIOUS OR ANTAGONISTIC OF HIM...AND HE'D USUALLY WIN THEM OVER TO HIS WAY OF THINKING.
HOW DID HE DO THIS?
Hitler used a special trick to get people to agree with him. He simply made them think that doing things his way would demonstrate the correctness of their own principles and ideas.

WHENEVER ANYONE WAS PRESENTED TO HIM, HITLER GAVE THEM THE SAME HYPNOTIC STARE FROM HIS SLIGHTLY PROTRUDING BLUE EYES. THIS MADE PEOPLE THINK THAT HE HAD SPECIAL, EVEN SUPERNATURAL POWERS - THAT HE WAS GERMANY'S MAN OF DESTINY.

WE'VE SEEN THAT IN 1923 HITLER'S ATTEMPT TO SEIZE POWER FAILED. BY 1929, HOWEVER, MANY THINGS HAD CHANGED FOR THE WORSE IN GERMANY. NOW THERE WERE FAR MORE PEOPLE IN THE COUNTRY WHO'D LOST ALL HOPE IN THE FUTURE AND DESPERATELY WANTED TO BELIEVE IN A SAVIOR - A MAGIC MAN WHO'D MAKE ALL THEIR PROBLEMS DISAPPEAR.

THE PHENOMENON OF NAZISM

WHAT EXACTLY WAS NAZISM?

THE PHENOMENON HAD MANY ROOTS. IT WAS A MIX OF VARIOUS IDEAS AND ATTITUDES BORROWED FROM PRUSSIAN MILITARISM, BISMARCK'S CONSERVATIVE AND OPPORTUNISTIC POLITICS (HE WAS THE STATESMAN WHO HAD UNITED GERMANY IN 1871), EXTREME NATIONALISM, MYSTICISM, ATHEISM, AND INSANE RACIST THEORIES BASED ON SOCIAL-DARWINISM, A THEORY THEN POPULAR THAT SAID ONLY THE STRONG MUST SURVIVE.

Put all this in a pot and stir, and many Germans honestly believed that the future of humanity lay in the triumph of the superior Aryan race over "subhumans" like Jews and Slavs.

Der Untermensch

HITLER'S CONCEPTION OF THE ARYAN RACE EXCLUDED THE VAST MAJORITY OF SLAVS FROM BEING PART CF THE "MASTER RACE", REGARDING SLAVS AS PEOPLE WHO HAD "VERY DANGEROUS JEWISH AND ASIATIC INFLUENCES". THE SLAVS WERE "SUB-HUMANS" - *UNTERMENSCHEN.*

A significant ideological influence on the Nazis was the 19th century German nationalist, Johann Fichte.
Fichte's works were an inspiration to Hitler and the Nazis.

WHO WAS THIS **FICHTE?**

LIVING DURING NAPOLEONIC FRANCE'S OCCUPATION OF BERLIN, FICHTE CALLED FOR A GERMAN NATIONAL REVOLUTION AGAINST THE FRENCH OCCUPIERS. HE MADE PASSIONATE PUBLIC SPEECHES, URGED HIS STUDENTS TO FIGHT THE FRENCH, AND STRESSED THE NEED FOR ACTION BY THE GERMAN NATION TO FREE ITSELF. FICHTE'S NATIONALISM WAS "BOTTOM-UP", POPULIST, AND OPPOSED TO THE TRADITIONAL ELITES.

We Germans need a *volkskrieg* or "people's war" against the French. We also need to purge the German language of all French words!
FICHTE'S *VÖLKISCH* NATIONALISM DENOUNCED SOULLESS MATERIALISM, INDIVIDUALISM, AND SECULARIZED, URBAN AND INDUSTRIAL SOCIETY.
What?! Soulless materialism and individualism, I sorta get. But what's a "secularized society"?
That's a society that's not based on religious education or the control of a church. In other words, it's a society whose laws and way of life isn't ecclesiastical.
Fichte's *Völkisch* nationalism praised the virtues of village life.
MOOO
FICHTE ADVOCATED A "SUPERIOR" SOCIETY BASED ON ETHNIC GERMAN "FOLK" CULTURE AND GERMAN "BLOOD". IT DENOUNCED ALL FOREIGNERS AND FOREIGN IDEAS AND DECLARED THAT JEWS, NATIONAL MINORITIES, CATHOLICS AND FREEMASONS WERE "TRAITORS TO THE NATION" AND UNWORTHY OF INCLUSION.

FICHTE CONDEMNED THE NEGLECT OF TRADITION AND DECAY OF MORALS, HE DENOUNCED THE DESTRUCTION OF THE NATURAL ENVIRONMENT, AND ALSO CRITICIZED "COSMOPOLITAN" CULTURES LIKE THE JEWS AND ROMA (GYPSIES).

HE ACCUSED THE JEWS IN GERMANY OF ALWAYS HAVING BEEN A "STATE WITHIN A STATE" THAT THREATENED GERMAN NATIONAL UNITY. HE PROPOSED TWO SOLUTIONS TO THIS "PROBLEM": THE FIRST WAS THE CREATION OF A JEWISH STATE IN PALESTINE TO FORCE THE JEWS TO LEAVE EUROPE. THE OTHER OPTION WAS VIOLENCE AGAINST JEWS.

Fichte's ideas were very popular among the Nazis. If there was one German philosopher the Nazis admired most, it was this guy Fichte.
GERMAN

Our goal should be to cut off all their heads in one night, and set new ones on their shoulders, which shouldn't contain a single Jewish idea.
Dude, you okay in the the head?

NAZISM ALSO HAD A PRACTICAL EXAMPLE TO FOLLOW: MUSSOLINI'S ITALIAN FASCISM WITH ITS PROMISE OF A "THIRD WAY" BETWEEN CAPITALISM AND SOCIALISM.

Nazism, fascism...it's all so confusing!
Let's take fascism first. The word comes from the Latin word *fasces,* a bundle of rods tied around an axe - the symbol of authority that officials held in ancient Rome.

FASCISMO E LIBERTÀ
SOME NAZIS, ESPECIALLY MORE RADICAL ONES LIKE **GREGOR STRASSER, JOSEPH GOEBBELS** AND **HEINRICH HIMMLER,** REJECTED ITALIAN FASCISM.
Fascism's too capitalist and too conservative.

THROUGHOUT THE RELATIONSHIP BETWEEN NAZI GERMANY AND FASCIST ITALY, A NUMBER OF LOWER-RANKING NAZIS SCORNFULLY VIEWED FASCISM AS A CONSERVATIVE MOVEMENT THAT DIDN'T HAVE A FULL REVOLUTIONARY POTENTIAL.

THE NAZIS WANTED EVERYONE TO UNITE UNDER THEIR FLAG TO FIGHT JEWS, SLAVS, AND COMMUNISTS. THEY INSISTED ON THIS UNION - EVEN BETWEEN GROUPS IN SOCIETY THAT WERE NATURALLY OPPOSED TO EACH OTHER - LIKE WORKERS AND CAPITALISTS, SHOPKEEPERS AND THEIR CUSTOMERS, FARMERS AND URBAN HOUSEWIVES, AND SO ON.

What problem did farmers and housewives have with each other?
The farmer wants to sell produce at a high price, and the housewife wants to buy cheap.

BOTH FASCISM AND NAZISM TRIED TO UNITE SOCIETY UNDER A SINGLE-PARTY DICTATORSHIP LED BY A SINGLE RULER.

THEY ATTEMPTED TO UNITE NATURAL OPPOSITES, LIKE WORKERS AND CAPITALISTS. THEY PROMISED EVERYTHING TO EVERYONE, LIKE HIGH PROFITS TO CAPITALISTS AND HIGH WAGES TO WORKERS. IT'S NO COINCIDENCE THAT THE *FASCES*, THE SYMBOL OF FASCISM, STANDS FOR THE UNITY OF VERY DIFFERENT SOCIO-ECONOMIC GROUPS AND LAYERS IN SOCIETY.

WAS THIS "UNION OF OPPOSITES" THAT BOTH NAZISM AND FASCISM STROVE TO ACHIEVE ACTUALLY POSSIBLE?

Don't high profits come from low wages, and don't high wages lead to smaller profits for the capitalist?
You just can't have both high wages and the highest possible profits at the same time.

SO WHAT *IS* THE DIFFERENCE BETWEEN FASCISM AND NAZISM?

THE MAIN DIFFERENCE WAS THAT UNLIKE THE ITALIAN FASCISTS, THE GERMAN NAZIS HAD A STRONG TRADITION OF PRUSSIAN MILITARY BLOODY-MINDEDNESS, AND CRAZY RACIST THEORIES THAT SAID "SUPERIOR" ARYANS MUST RULE OVER OTHER RACES.

THE CONCEPT OF THE ARYAN RACE, WHICH THE NAZIS PROMOTED, STEMS FROM RACIAL THEORIES THAT SAY THAT EUROPEANS ARE THE DESCENDANTS OF INDO-IRANIAN SETTLERS, PEOPLE OF ANCIENT INDIA AND ANCIENT PERSIA.

SUPPORTERS OF THIS THEORY BASE THEIR VIEWS ON THE SIMILARITY OF EUROPEAN WORDS TO INDO-IRANIAN LANGUAGES.

The German philosopher Johann Gottfried Herder argued that the Germanic peoples have close racial connec-tions with the ancient Indians and ancient Persians.

Johann Gottfried Herder

HERDER CLAIMED THE ANCIENT INDIANS AND PERSIANS WERE ADVANCED PEOPLES WITH A GREAT CAPACITY FOR NOBILITY, WISDOM, RESTRAINT AND SCIENCE.

HOLY
COW

I can see where this nutty argument's going. Herder, and of course the Nazis, make a distinction between what they see as "high and noble" Aryan culture and "parasitic" Semitic culture.

It's our fault again?

IN THE 19TH CENTURY, WHITE SUPREMACISTS ARGUED THAT WHITE PEOPLE WERE MEMBERS OF AN ARYAN "MASTER RACE" "SUPERIOR" TO OTHER RACES, ESPECIALLY THE SEMITIC RACE.

THE FRENCH ARISTOCRAT AND RACIAL THEORIST **ARTHUR DE GOBINEAU** BLAMED THE FALL OF THE *ANCIEN RÉGIME* IN FRANCE DURING THE REVOLUTION OF 1789-1793 ON "DEGENERACY" CAUSED BY THE INTERMIXING OF RACES.

The mixing of races destroyed the purity of the Aryan race!

Arthur de Gobineau

GOBINEAU'S THEORIES, WHICH HAD MANY SUPPORTERS IN GERMANY, STRESSED THE "IRRECONCILABLE DIFFERENCES" BETWEEN ARYAN AND JEWISH CULTURES.

ARYAN MYSTICISM CLAIMED THAT CHRISTIANITY ORIGINATED IN ARYAN RELIGIOUS TRADITION AND THAT JEWS HAD USURPED THE LEGEND FROM ARYANS.

A clever but false argument to get around the fact that Jesus Christ was a Jew!

Houston Stewart Chamberlain

HOUSTON STEWART CHAMBERLAIN, AN ENGLISH PROPONENT OF RACIAL THEORY, SUPPORTED NOTIONS OF GERMANIC SUPREMACY AND ANTI-SEMITISM IN GERMANY. HIS BOOK, PUBLISHED IN 1899, *FOUNDATIONS OF THE NINETEENTH CENTURY,* PRAISED GERMANIC PEOPLES FOR THEIR CREATIVITY AND IDEALISM, WHILE ASSERTING THAT THE GOOD GERMANIC SPIRIT WAS THREATENED BY A NEGATIVE "JEWISH" SPIRIT OF SELFISHNESS AND MATERIALISM.

His book became popular, especially in Germany.
Chamberlain used his thesis to support the conservatism of monarchies and to denounce such ideas as democracy, liberalism, and socialism.

CHAMBERLAIN STRESSED THE NEED OF A NATION TO MAINTAIN RACIAL PURITY IN ORDER TO PREVENT "DEGENERATION", AND ARGUED THAT RACIAL INTERMINGLING WITH JEWS MUST NEVER BE PERMITTED.

In 1923, Chamberlain met Hitler, whom he admired as a leader.
THE PROTOCOLS OF THE ELDERS OF ZION, PUBLISHED IN 1912, WAS AN ANTISEMITIC FORGERY CREATED BY THE POLICE OF THE RUSSIAN EMPIRE. THE PROTOCOLS CLAIMED THAT THERE EXISTED A SECRET INTERNATIONAL JEWISH CONSPIRACY TO TAKE OVER THE WHOLE WORLD.
Who believed this garbage?
People with garbage in their hearts and minds.
PEACE
ANTISEMITES BELIEVED (MANY STILL DO!) THAT THE PROTOCOLS OF THE ELDERS OF ZION WERE REAL.

Slow down a bit. What's a protocol? And who's this Zion?
A protocol's an original draft of an official document. Zion's a hill in ancient Jerusalem, the royal residence of King David; it also means heaven for the Jews.
THE PROTOCOLS OF THE ELDERS OF ZION BECAME WIDELY POPULAR AFTER WORLD WAR ONE.
HITLER WAS INTRODUCED TO THE PROTOCOLS BY THE "THEORETICIAN" OF THE NAZI PARTY, ALFRED ROSENBERG.
FROM 1920 ONWARD, HITLER CLAIMED THAT JUDAISM AND MARXISM WERE VERY CLOSELY CONNECTED.
The Jews and Bolsheviks are one and the same. Marxism's a Jewish ideology.
Darwin was British. Does that make Darwinism a British theory?

RADICAL ANTISEMITISM WAS PROMOTED BY PROMINENT ADVOCATES OF *VÖLKISCH* NATIONALISM, INCLUDING **EUGEN DIEDERICHS, PAUL DE LAGARDE**, AND **JULIUS LANGBEHN**.

Eugen Diederichs

Paul De Lagarde

Julius Langbehn

THESE THREE "WISE MEN" CALLED FOR THE ANNIHILATION AND EXTERMINATION OF ALL JEWS BECAUSE THEY "POLLUTED" THE CULTURES OF DIFFERENT NATIONS AND "DESTROYED FAITH" WITH THEIR SO-CALLED "MATERIALISTIC LIBERALISM".

What rot! What nasty nonsense these anti-Semites spewed!

We published Langbehn's ideas and gave them to our soldiers on the front during WWII.

THE NAZIS USED THE "STAB-IN-THE-BACK" MYTH TO ACCUSE JEWS OF NOT BEING TRUE GERMAN PATRIOTS. NATURALLY, THIS INTENSIFIED ANTISEMITISM IN GERMANY.

The ***Judenfrage***, or "Jewish Question", is a staple in Nazi propaganda. They use it to whip up hatred against us.

NAZISM'S RACIAL IDEAS WERE ALSO BASED ON THE THEORIES OF 19TH CENTURY FRENCH BIOLOGIST **JEAN-BAPTISTE LAMARCK.**

UNLIKE DARWIN, LAMARCK RANKED ALL RACES IN A HIERARCHY OF EVOLUTION FROM APES.

Jean-Baptiste Lamarck

Darwin's theory didn't grade races in a hierarchy of higher or lower evolution from apes.
That's right. Darwin simply said all humans evolved from us.

SUPPORTER OF LAMARCKIAN THEORY ARGUED THAT "LOWER" RACES HAD BEEN EXPOSED TO EXTREMELY DIFFICULT CONDITIONS FAR TOO LONG FOR THEM TO BE ABLE TO IMPROVE.

THE RACIAL THEORIST **ERNST HAECKEL** USED LAMARCKIAN THEORY TO DESCRIBE THE EXISTENCE OF A STRUGGLE BETWEEN DIFFERENT RACES.

HAECKEL PLACED ALL RACES ON A HIERARCHY OF EVOLUTION FROM WHOLLY HUMAN TO SUBHUMAN.

Ernst Haeckel

I thought it was the *other way round* - the easier the conditions, the lazier and stupider you become.

THE NAZIS ALSO BORROWED IDEAS FROM THE WELL-KNOWN GENETICIST **GREGOR MENDEL**.

Gregor Mendel

THEY ARGUED THAT GENETIC TRAITS AND ATTRIBUTES WERE PASSED ON FROM ONE GENERATION TO ANOTHER.

Biological illnesses are sometimes transferred from parents to children, but the racialists, I mean *racists*, say social traits are also inherited from one's parents. That's a stretch!
I see.

BASING THEIR ARGUMENTS ON MENDELIAN THEORY, THE NAZIS CLAIMED THAT RACE WAS BEHIND TRAITS SUCH AS INVENTIVENESS OR CRIMINAL BEHAVIOR.

DURING WORLD WAR ONE, GERMAN SOCIOLOGIST **JOHANN PLENGE** SPOKE OF THE RISE OF A "NATIONAL SOCIALISM" IN GERMANY WHICH WOULD USE WHAT HE CALLED THE "IDEAS OF 1914" THAT WERE HOSTILE TO THE "IDEAS OF 1789" -THE FRENCH REVOLUTION, THE RIGHTS OF MAN, LIBERALISM, DEMOCRACY AND INDIVIDUALISM.

THE "IDEAS OF 1914" INCLUDED "GERMAN VALUES" OF DUTY, DISCIPLINE, LAW, AND ORDER.

Sorry...I couldn't find a picture of him.
Johann Plenge

He rejected the French Revolution!

What could be more honorable that the spirit that led us into WWI?

Man, what've you been smoking?

Plenge rejected the idea of unlimited freedom.

PLENGE BELIEVED THAT ETHNIC SOLIDARITY (*VOLKSGEMEINSCHAFT*) WOULD REPLACE CLASS DIVISION AND CLASS STRUGGLE, AND THAT "RACIAL COMRADES" WOULD UNITE TO CREATE SOCIALISM IN THE STRUGGLE OF "PROLETARIAN" GERMANY AGAINST "CAPITALIST" GREAT BRITAIN.

HE WANTED AN ECONOMY WHICH WOULD SERVE THE WHOLE OF GERMANY UNDER THE LEADERSHIP OF THE STATE. THIS NATIONAL SOCIALISM WAS OPPOSED TO CAPITALISM, WHICH HE BELIEVED PROMOTED SELFISHNESS AND INDIVIDUALISM, BOTH HARMFUL TO GERMANY'S "NATIONAL INTEREST".

We Germans need an authoritarian rational ruling elite to develop national socialism through a hierarchical and technocratic state.

These ideas formed an important part of Nazism.

ANOTHER MAJOR INFLUENCE ON NAZISM WAS THE GERMAN CULTURAL PHILOSOPHER, **OSWALD SPENGLER.**

AFTER 1933 SPENGLER BECAME ALIENATED FROM NAZISM AND WAS LATER CONDEMNED BY THE NAZIS FOR CRITICIZING ADOLF HITLER. STILL, HIS CONCEPTION OF NATIONAL SOCIALISM WAS SHARED BY THE NAZIS.

Oswald Spengler

We Italian fascists also like Spengler's ideas!

Italian dictator Benito Mussolini

SPENGLER'S BOOK *THE DECLINE OF THE WEST*, WAS PUBLISHED IN 1918 DURING THE FINAL MONTHS OF WWI. IT TALKED ABOUT THE DECADENCE OF MODERN EUROPEAN CIVILIZATION, ITSELF THE RESULT OF INDIVIDUALISM AND COSMOPOLITANISM.

You lost me there, pal. What on earth's cosmo-politanism?
Cosmopolitan means common to all the world, being at home in any part of the world, free from national prejudices.

SPENGLER'S MAIN THESIS WAS THAT A LAW OF HISTORICAL DEVELOPMENT OF CULTURES EXISTS. THIS INVOLVES A CYCLE OF BIRTH, MATURITY, AGING, AND DEATH, WHEN A CULTURE REACHES ITS FINAL FORM OF CIVILIZATION, LOSES ITS CREATIVE CAPACITY, AND SUCCUMBS TO DECADENCE UNTIL THE EMERGENCE OF "BARBARIANS" CREATES A NEW EPOCH.

HE BELIEVED THAT THE "YOUNG" GERMAN NATION AS AN IMPERIAL POWER WOULD INHERIT THE LEGACY OF ANCIENT ROME, LEAD A RESTORATION OF VALUE IN "BLOOD" AND INSTINCT, WHILE THE IDEALS OF LOGIC AND RATIONALISM WOULD BE SHOWN TO BE COMPLETELY RIDICULOUS AND ABSURD.

The western world has succumbed to intellectual decadence, money, cosmopolitan, urban and irreligious life, selfish individualism, biological and spiritual infertility.
Wow, really?

SPENGLER'S IDEAS OF "PRUSSIAN SOCIALISM", WHICH HE SET FORTH IN HIS 1919 BOOK *PREUSSENTUM UND SOZIALISMUS,* ALSO INFLUENCED NAZISM.
The meaning of socialism is that life is controlled not by the opposition between rich and poor, but by the rank that achievement and talent bestow. That is our freedom, freedom from the economic despotism of the individual.
LIKE PLENGE, SPENGLER ADVOCATED A NATIONAL SOCIALISM THAT WAS FREE FROM MARXISM AND THAT WOULD CONNECT THE INDIVIDUAL TO THE STATE THROUGH CORPORATIST ORGANIZATION.
Come again?
A corporation is a united body, a company or association for commercial or other purposes. He means that under national socialism people will be organized in units that resemble corporations.

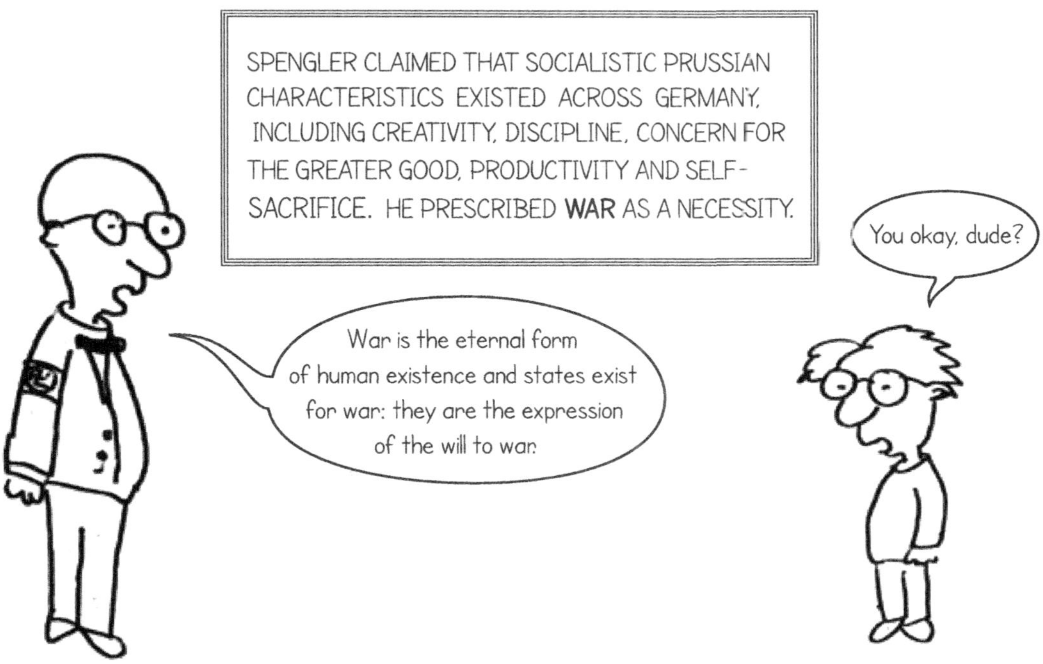
SPENGLER CLAIMED THAT SOCIALISTIC PRUSSIAN CHARACTERISTICS EXISTED ACROSS GERMANY, INCLUDING CREATIVITY, DISCIPLINE, CONCERN FOR THE GREATER GOOD, PRODUCTIVITY AND SELF-SACRIFICE. HE PRESCRIBED **WAR** AS A NECESSITY.
You okay, dude?
War is the eternal form of human existence and states exist for war: they are the expression of the will to war.

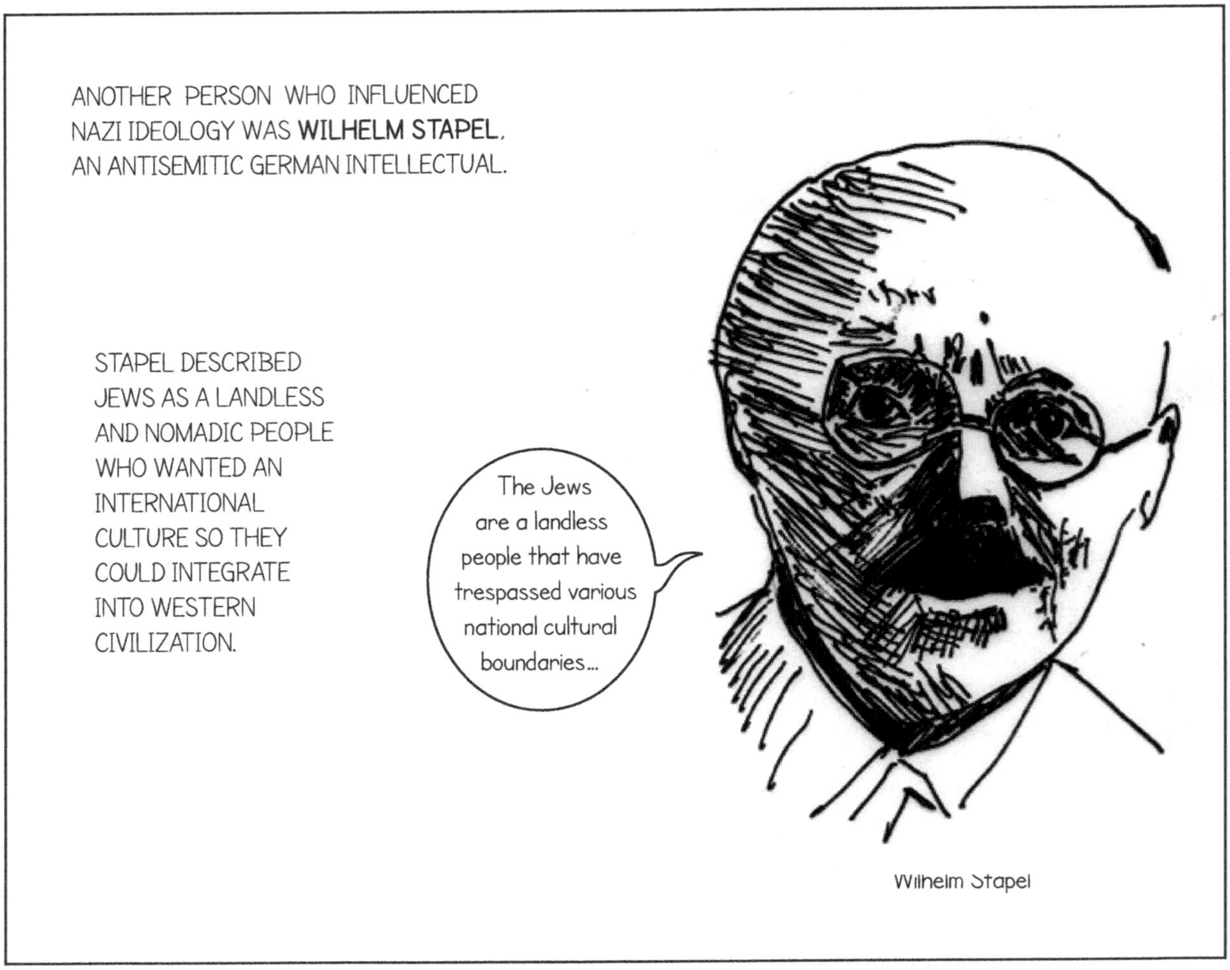
ANOTHER PERSON WHO INFLUENCED NAZI IDEOLOGY WAS **WILHELM STAPEL**, AN ANTISEMITIC GERMAN INTELLECTUAL.
STAPEL DESCRIBED JEWS AS A LANDLESS AND NOMADIC PEOPLE WHO WANTED AN INTERNATIONAL CULTURE SO THEY COULD INTEGRATE INTO WESTERN CIVILIZATION.
The Jews are a landless people that have trespassed various national cultural boundaries...
Wilhelm Stapel

I don't buy Stapel's arguments. There are plenty of Jews who aren't landless, including big capitalists. How can you generalize about an entire race and ignore what class they belong to?
And what's wrong with being landless?

FINALLY, A GUY CALLED **ARTHUR MOELLER VAN DEN BRUCK** INFLUENCED THE NAZIS. HE REJECTED REACTIONARY CONSERVATISM, AND PROPOSED A NEW KIND OF STATE HE CALLED THE "**THIRD *REICH***" THAT WOULD UNITE ALL ECONOMIC CLASSES IN SOCIETY UNDER STRICT AUTHORITARIAN RULE.
I propose a joining of the nationalism of the right with the socialism of the left!
NAZISM REJECTED THE MARXIST CONCEPT OF CLASS STRUGGLE. INSTEAD, IT PROMOTED THE IDEA OF *VOLKSGEMEINSCHAFT*, OR "NATIONAL COMMUNITY".
Arthur Moeller Van Den Bruck

IN THE 1920S, HITLER URGED THE NAZIS TO UNITE IN OPPOSITION TO "JEWISH MARXISM".
The three vices of Jewish Marxism are democracy, pacifism and internationalism.
What kind of a socialist are you?

HITLER INSISTED THAT FOR THE NAZIS THE TERM "SOCIALIST" HAD NOTHING TO DO WITH MARXIST SOCIALISM.

NEITHER FASCISM NOR NAZISM CHALLENGED PRIVATE PROPERTY, THE PRINCIPLE WITHOUT WHICH CAPITALISM ISN'T POSSIBLE.

Marxism is anti-property. True socialism isn't. I absolutely insist on protecting private property and encouraging private initiative.
And another thing! businessmen know nothing except their profit. "Fatherland" is but a word for them. I'm disgusted with the ruling elites of Germany in the Weimar Republic. They are cowardly @#its!

THE NAZIS WANTED TO OVERCOME SOCIAL DIVISIONS, WHICH THEY THOUGHT ARTIFICIAL. THEY BELIEVED THAT ALL PARTS OF A RACIALLY HOMOGENOUS SOCIETY OUGHT TO CO-OPERATE IN THE NAME OF NATIONAL UNITY.

In our national socialist society, the state will control and set wage levels.

NAZISM DENOUNCED BOTH CAPITALISM AND COMMUNISM FOR BEING ASSOCIATED WITH "JEWISH MATERIALISM". LIKE OTHER FASCIST MOVEMENTS, NAZISM OUTLAWED STRIKES BY WORKERS AND LOCKOUTS BY EMPLOYERS BECAUSE THEY SAW THESE AS A THREAT TO NATIONAL UNITY.

BY SUPPORTING THE UNION OF SOCIAL GROUPS WHOSE INTERESTS ARE NORMALLY COMPLETELY OPPOSED TO EACH OTHER - WORKERS AND CAPITALISTS, SHOPKEEPERS AND CUSTOMERS, FARMERS AND HOUSEWIVES, SOCIALISTS AND NATIONALISTS - THE NAZIS WERE CREATING A VERY EXPLOSIVE AND DANGEROUS SOCIETY.

I just don't get how both workers *and* bosses can be happy?
Yeah, how can you have high wages *and* big profits at one and the same time?
This would only work if you did it at the expense of people living in other countries.

THE ONLY WAY FOR A FASCIST OR NAZI SYSTEM TO WORK IS FOR IT TO STEAL AND PLUNDER THE WEALTH OF OTHER COUNTRIES.

FASCISM AND NAZISM ARE LIKE FUSION BOMBS THAT MUST EXPLODE IN WARS OF CONQUEST BECAUSE THE SOCIAL FORCES THEY TRY TO UNITE CAN ONLY COEXIST IF THERE'S ENOUGH WEALTH TO MAKE EVERYONE HAPPY.

Fascism is born of capitalism in crisis. It is the last stand of capital in its struggle to defeat labor. It unites with the petty bourgeoisie while at the same time pretending to be revolutionary.

WITHIN THE NAZI PARTY THERE WERE PEOPLE WHO WERE MORE "SOCIALIST" THAN OTHERS, LIKE THE BROTHERS **OTTO** (ON THE LEFT BELOW) AND **GREGOR STRASSER.**

Otto Strasser

Gregor Strasser

MANY OF THE EX-SOLDIERS IN THE BROWNSHIRTS (S.A) WANTED THE NAZIS TO GET RID OF BIG CAPITALIST FIRMS.

The SA only went against big capital, not capital in general!

V.I. Lenin

ANOTHER RADICAL NAZI, PROPAGANDA MINISTER **JOSEPH GOEBBELS,** STRESSED THE SOCIALIST CHARACTER OF NAZISM, AND CLAIMED IN HIS DIARY THAT IF HE WERE TO PICK BETWEEN BOLSHEVISM AND CAPITALISM, HE'D PICK BOLSHEVISM.

It would be much better for us to go down with Bolshevism than live in eternal slavery under capitalism.

Joseph Goebbels

WHAT WAS HITLER'S "CONTRIBUTION" TO NAZISM, IF ANY?

IN HIS BOOK, *MEIN KAMPF,* HITLER HUMBLY PRESENTED A VERSION OF THE EARLIEST YEARS OF THE NAZI PARTY DURING THE FIRST TENTATIVE MEETINGS OF THE GROUP IN 1919.

THE IMAGE HE CREATED WAS OF A HOUNDED TEAM OF GOOD GERMAN PATRIOTS WHOSE VERY LIVES WERE THREATENED BY THE "JEWISH-BOLSHEVIK MENACE" THEY WERE TRYING TO GO AGAINST.

The members wanted to appear in public as little as possible, for fear of being beaten up. In their mind's eye they already saw the first great meeting smashed and the movement finished for good. I had a hard time putting forward my opinion that we must not dodge this struggle, but prepare for it, and for this reason acquire the armament which alone offers protection against violence. Terror is not broken by the mind, but by terror. The success of the first meeting strengthened my position in this respect. We gained courage for a second meeting on a somewhat larger scale.

IN *MEIN KAMPF* HITLER SAID THAT THE TRUE BASIS OF THE STATE WASN'T CLASS INTEREST. THE STATE FOR HIM DIDN'T REPRESENT THE INTERESTS OF THE STRONGEST CLASS IN SOCIETY, WHICH IN A CAPITALIST SOCIETY ARE THE CAPITALISTS. HITLER DIDN'T BELIEVE THAT THIS STATE'S BASIC ROLE IS TO PROTECT THE INTERESTS OF THE RICH AGAINST THE POOR.

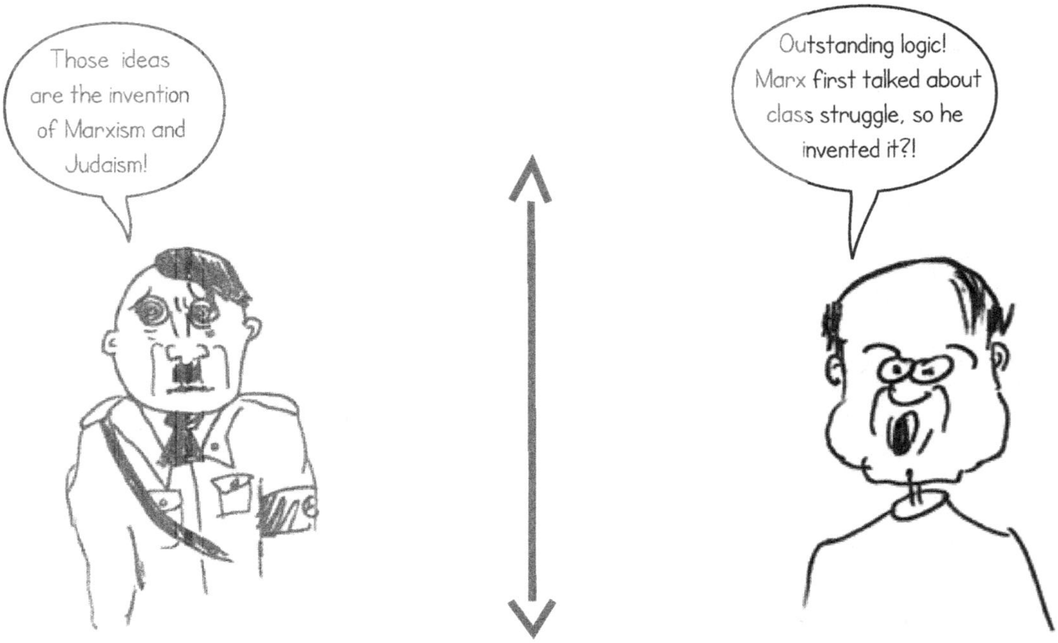
Those ideas are the invention of Marxism and Judaism!
Outstanding logic! Marx first talked about class struggle, so he invented it?!

Fascism and Nazism pretend to be anti-capitalist while in reality being anti-worker. They do this to attract more people.

SIEG
oder
BOLSCHE
WISMUS

This Nazi poster reads "Victory over Boshevism".

Respectable conservatives initially shun the brutality of the fascists, but when they're threatened by revolution, they run to the fascists for protection.
Oh, you *annoying* Communists!

FOR HITLER, THE MAIN DUTY OF THE GERMAN STATE WAS TO UNITE WITHIN ITS BORDERS ALL GERMANS, AND TO ELIMINATE ALIEN ELEMENTS THAT MIGHT CORRUPT THE "PURE" GERMAN RACE.

Did you know that in 1933 in Germany there were only around 523,000 Jews out of a population of 67 million?

HITLER BELIEVED ALL OF GERMANY'S PROBLEMS WERE THE WORK OF AN "INTERNATIONAL JEWISH CONSPIRACY". FROM THIS ILLOGICAL THESIS BASED ON *THE PROTOCOLS OF THE ELDERS OF ZION* IT "FOLLOWED" THAT THE GERMAN STATE HAD TO PROVIDE ENOUGH RESOURCES AND "LIVING SPACE", OR ***LEBENSRAUM***, TO GERMANS. THEREFORE, SINCE THE STATE EXISTED TO PROMOTE THE WELL-BEING OF ITS PEOPLE, IT WAS PERFECTLY NORMAL AND LEGITIMATE FOR THE STATE TO GRAB THIS "LIVING SPACE" FROM NEIGHBORING RACES.

History proves that the German people owe their existence solely to their determination to fight in the east and to get land by military conquest. Land in Europe is only to be gained at the expense of Russia.
We'll see about that, you racist!
SOVIET RED ARMY

THE SOVIET LEADERSHIP READ *MEIN KAMPF* VERY CAREFULLY, AND TOOK INTO ACCOUNT THE PLANS HITLER SET OUT IN IT: WIPE OUT MARXIST IDEOLOGY AND GRAB LAND FROM SLAVS, ESPECIALLY RUSSIANS AND UKRAINIANS.

HITLER DESCRIBED SLAVS AS "A MASS OF BORN SLAVES."

THE NAZI BELIEF IN SLAVIC "INFERIORITY" SERVED TO LEGITIMIZE THEIR GOAL OF *LEBENSRAUM* FOR ALL GERMANS IN EASTERN EUROPE. HITLER'S PLAN WAS FOR MILLIONS OF GERMANIC PEOPLES TO MOVE INTO THE CONQUERED TERRITORIES OF EASTERN EUROPE, WHILE THE SLAVS THERE WERE TO BE KILLED, REMOVED, OR ENSLAVED.

The Treaty of Brest-Litovsk of March 1918, when Soviet Russia surrendered huge areas of land to Germany, was my kind of treaty.

IN HIS EARLY YEARS AS LEADER OF THE N.S.D.A.P. HITLER SAID HE'D ACCEPT FRIENDLY RELATIONS WITH RUSSIA ON THE CONDITION THAT RUSSIA RETURN TO THE BORDERS SET BY THE TREATY OF BREST-LITOVSK OF 1918.

We'll see in the next book of this series that in WWII Hitler clung to the hope that the British would join him against the Soviet Union.

HIS ATTITUDES CHANGED BY THE END OF 1922, WHEN HE SUPPORTED THE IDEA OF AN ALLIANCE OF GERMANY WITH GREAT BRITAIN TO DESTROY RUSSIA.

HITLER LATER EXPLAINED HOW FAR INTO RUSSIA HE INTENDED THE THIRD *REICH* TO EXPAND:

"Asia, what a disquieting reservoir of men! The safety of Europe will not be assured until we have driven Asia back behind the Urals. No organized Russian state must be allowed to exist west of that line."

Hitler wanted to turn Russia into what India was for the British.

THE *LEBENSRAUM* POLICY PLANNED THE MASS EXPANSION OF GERMANY EASTWARDS TO THE THE URAL MOUNTAINS. HITLER WANTED THE "SURPLUS" RUSSIAN POPULATION LIVING WEST OF THE URALS TO BE DEPORTED TO THE EAST.

WHAT ELSE DID HITLER SAY IN *MEIN KAMPF*?

He added a big dose of his megalomaniacal **egoism!**

HITLER INTRODUCED THE "**LEADER PRINCIPLE**" OR ***FÜHRERPRINZIP***. THIS MEANT THAT EVERYONE IN THE DIFFERENT LEVELS OF THE NAZI PARTY HAD TO BLINDLY OBEY THEIR SUPERIORS IN THE HIERARCHY. THEY ALSO SWORE PERSONAL LOYALTY TO HITLER.

AT THE APEX OF THIS PYRAMID OF POWER WAS NATURALLY HITLER HIMSELF. SOUNDS A LITTLE UNDEMOCRATIC? NONETHELESS, FOR THE GERMANS, WHO NEVER HAD MUCH OF A TRADITION OF DEMOCRACY, THIS IDEA WAS APPEALING.

OTTO STRASSER CRITICIZED THE *FÜHRERPRINZIP* AS HAVING BEEN CREATED BY BENITO MUSSOLINI.
The *Führerprinzip* is a foreign, imported idea. It has no place in Nazism.

The *Führerprinzip* will evolve into a huge cult of personality built upon the myth of Hitler as the personification of Nietzsche's ***übermensch*** or "Superior Man".
THE ***FÜHRERPRINZIP*** WAS A CONVENIENT PRINCIPLE FOR THE NAZIS. IT ALLOWED THE PARTY TO WEATHER CHANGES IN ORGANIZATIONAL PRIORITIES WITHOUT HAVING IDEOLOGICAL DEBATES AND ADMINISTRATIVE CHAOS TO DEAL WITH.

The *Führerprinzip* set the NSDAP apart from all other political rivals, especially the more democratic ones on the left.
THE MAIN IDEA WAS THAT THE LEADER'S POWER MUST OVERRIDE ANY AND ALL DECISION-MAKING IN THE NAZI PARTY.

MORE THAN ANY OTHER FACTOR, IT WAS THIS ORGANIZATIONAL ADVANTAGE - REINFORCED BY HITLER'S SELF-CREATED MYTH OF THE WOULD-BE *FÜHRER* AS A SUPERIOR TYPE OF *HOMO SAPIENS* - THAT ALLOWED THE N.S.D.A.P TO RISE FROM POLITICAL INSIGNIFICANCE TO ELECTORAL SUPERIORITY IN WEIMAR GERMANY.

THE ATTRACTION OF THE NAZIS

IN ORDER TO DRAW SUPPORTERS, WHENEVER ADOLF HITLER SPOKE, HE FOCUSSED ON SUCH VAGUE IDEAS AS "FATHERLAND", "THE GREAT GERMAN *VOLK*", "SACRIFICE", "HONOR", "BLOOD", AND "LOYALTY".

THERE WAS A **NEGATIVE GLUE** IN NAZISM'S MAIN **TARGETS OF HATE: THE TREATY OF VERSAILLES, THE WEIMAR REPUBLIC, PARLIAMENTARY DEMOCRACY, MARXISM AND JUDAISM.** ALL THESE WERE ATTACKED.

The Nazi movement was like a hate club with enough targets to keep all its members happy.
Hate's fun for *homo stupidus.*

LET'S TALK A LITTLE MORE ABOUT WHO WAS DRAWN TO THIS CRACK-BRAINED, HATE-FILLED MOVEMENT.

A 1923 SURVEY OF 5,000 NAZI PARTY MEMBERS SHOWED THAT 60 PERCENT WERE FROM THE LOWER MIDDLE URBAN CLASS: TRADESMEN, SHOPKEEPERS, CLERKS AND MINOR OFFICIALS.

THESE PEOPLE LOOKED UP WITH ENVY AND HOSTILITY TO THE RICH CAPITALISTS, AND WITH ANGER AND FEAR AT THOSE BELOW THEM ON THE SOCIAL LADDER, THE WAGE-EARNING WORKERS.

DURING THE RELATIVE STABILITY OF 1924-29, THE LOWER MIDDLE CLASS WEREN'T ALIENATED OR ANGRY ENOUGH TO BE ATTRACTED BY THE NAZIS.

The Nazis were rejuvenated by the renewed economic crisis following the Wall Street Crash in October 1929.
Yup.

IN 1928 THE PARTY HAD 40,000 MEMBERS, GOT ABOUT ONE MILLION VOTES AND WON 12 SEATS IN PARLIAMENT. AFTER THE WORLD FINANCIAL CRISIS HIT, THINGS CHANGED IN FAVOR OF THE NAZIS. BY 1932 THEY HAD 800,000 MEMBERS, 16.5 MILLION VOTES AND 230 SEATS IN THE *REICHSTAG*.

We were impressed by the disciplined SA parades during a period when there was economic chaos, and everyone was depressed with no hope for the future.

ONCE THE GREAT DEPRESSION BEGAN, OTHER SOCIAL LAYERS WERE ATTRACTED TO THE HARDCORE NAZI BASE OF SUPPORT, THE URBAN LOWER MIDDLE CLASS.

My departure was the end of majority government.

Chancellor Hermann Muller

IN MARCH 1930, GERMANY'S LAST SOCIAL DEMOCRATIC CHANCELLOR, **HERMANN MULLER**, RESIGNED BECAUSE THE PARTIES OF THE CENTER (NEITHER TOO FAR TO THE RIGHT NOR LEFT) WERE TOTALLY UNABLE TO WORK TOGETHER.

WHO GOVERNED THE COUNTRY WHILE CENTRIST PARTIES TRIED, AND FAILED, TO CREATE A COALITION GOVERNMENT?

THIS TASK FELL INTO THE HANDS OF **PRESIDENT HINDENBURG** AND HIS ADVISORS, **GENERAL WILHELM GROENER** AND **GENERAL KURT VON SCHLEICHER**.

I may be old and senile, but as President I must find a Chancellor who can unite enough political parties to rule properly.

HINDENBURG AND THE MILITARY MEN AROUND HIM WERE LESS WORRIED ABOUT PROTECTING DEMOCRACY THAN DEALING WITH THE ECONOMIC CRISIS. THE MAN THEY CHOSE FOR CHANCELLOR WAS **HEINRICH BRÜNING** FROM THE CATHOLIC CENTER PARTY.

I'm a war veteran, a conservative, and I hate Social Democracy.

Heinrich Brüning

AT FIRST BRÜNING HAD SOME SUCCESS: HE WAS ABLE TO GET A SUSPENSION ON REPARATIONS PAYMENTS.

FROM 1930-1932, BRÜNING TRIED TO GOVERN WITHOUT A MAJORITY IN PARLIAMENT. HE DID THIS WITH THE PRESIDENT'S EMERGENCY DECREES.

Boo!

BRÜNING EXPECTED AND ACCEPTED THAT THE ECONOMIC CRISIS WOULD CONTINUE TO GET WORSE FOR A WHILE BEFORE THINGS IMPROVED.

Like a dictator!

THE GREAT DEPRESSION HIT ITS LOWEST POINT WHILE BRÜNING WAS CHANCELLOR.

IN LINE WITH THE CONSERVATIVE ECONOMIC THEORY THAT LESS GOVERNMENT SPENDING WOULD SPUR ECONOMIC GROWTH, BRÜNING DRASTICALLY CUT STATE EXPENDITURES, AND REDUCED SOCIAL SERVICES AND UNEMPLOYMENT BENEFITS.

HE SOON BECAME VERY UNPOPULAR FOR TACKLING THE ECONOMIC CRISIS IN THIS COLD-HEARTED MANNER.

We call Brüning the Hunger Chancellor!
And to add insult to injury, at a time when poor people need help most, Brüning's government keeps up subsidies to the large *Junker* farmers.

BRÜNING MADE A GRAVE POLITICAL ERROR WHEN, USING ARTICLE 48 OF THE CONSTITUTION, HE DISSOLVED THE *REICHSTAG* IN JULY 1930 IN THE HOPE OF GAINING A MAJORITY IN THE NEXT PARLIAMENTARY ELECTIONS IN SEPTEMBER. INSTEAD, THE COMMUNISTS DID VERY WELL AND GAINED A TOTAL OF 77 SEATS. HITLER'S NAZIS HOWEVER DID EVEN BETTER, AND THE N.S.D.A.P NOW BECAME THE SECOND PARTY IN GERMANY AFTER THE SOCIAL DEMOCRATS.

We Nazis got 107 seats in the election!

ON OCTOBER 11, 1931, IN THE TOWN OF HARZBURG, THE NAZIS FORMED AN ALLIANCE WITH THE RIGHT-WING GERMAN NATIONAL PEOPLE'S PARTY (D.N.V.P) AND OTHERS, SUCH AS PRO-MONARCHIST ARMY OFFICERS AND CERTAIN POWERFUL INDUSTRIALISTS.

This alliance was officially known as the "National Front", but most called it the *Harzburg Front*.

THE HARZBURG FRONT WAS STRONGLY OPPOSED TO THE YOUNG PLAN. ITS MEMBERS BELIEVED THAT FOLLOWING THE PLAN MEANT GERMANS WOULD HAVE TO WORK AS SLAVES FOR THREE GENERATIONS IN ORDER TO REPAY THE LOANS THAT WERE FORCED ON GERMANY.

Bis in die dritte Generation
müßt ihr fronen!

Why were these people against the Young Plan and good ol' Yankee greenbacks?
The Nazis didn't want to pay a single cent of the Versailles reparations bill. They believed the Young Plan was the work of a conspiracy of Jews to make Germans their economic slaves forever.

HITLER'S GREATEST OBSTACLE ON THE ROAD TO POWER WAS LACK OF MONEY.

Hate, hate, hate!

HE NEEDED TO LOOK AROUND AND FIND BIG WALLETS TO FINANCE HIS POLITICAL AMBITIONS. BUT THERE WAS A PROBLEM...

BETWEEN 1924 AND 1929, THE INDUSTRIALISTS (WHO'D BEEN PLEASED WITH THE PROGRESS STRESEMANN HAD MADE WITH THE GRADUAL LIQUIDATION OF THE TREATY OF VERSAILLES) DIDN'T WANT HIM RUNNING AROUND WHIPPING UP HATRED.

HITLER MANAGED TO GAIN THE SUPPORT OF THE LEADER OF THE NATIONALIST PARTY (D.N.V.P), **ALFRED HUGENBERG**, A FORMER DIRECTOR OF THE BIG KRUPPS ARMAMENTS COMPANY. DURING THE INFLATION OF 1923, HE'D BOUGHT A STRING OF NATIONAL AND LOCAL NEWSPAPERS, AND THE LARGE U.F.A FILM COMPANY WITH ITS MOVIE THEATERS AND NEWSREELS.

I now put this vast publicity machine at the service of Hitler.
Alfred Hugenberg

THE NAZIS ALSO GOT SUPPORT BY COOPERATING WITH SUCH PEOPLE AS **HJALMAR SCHACHT**, HEAD OF THE *REICHSBANK*, THE COUNTRY'S CENTRAL BANK, AND **FRANZ SELDTE**, LEADER OF THE ULTRA-PATRIOTIC ***STAHLHELM*** OR "STEEL HELMET" VETERANS' ORGANIZATION.

Hjalmar Schacht

Franz Seldte

NOW THE NAZIS BECAME THE MAIN REPRESENTATIVES OF NATIONALISM IN THE COUNTRY AND MOST BUSINESSMEN BEGAN TO SUPPORT HITLER AND HIS PARTY.

Marxismus

BIG BUSINESSMEN KNEW THAT IF CLASS WAR ERUPTED IN GERMANY, THE NAZIS WOULD BE ON THEIR SIDE AGAINST THE COMMUNISTS.

The German Communists were capable of making revolution?
Probably not, but rich Germans were afraid of them. People always tend to exaggerate the strength of their enemies.

5
5
Deutsches Reich

ANOTHER SOCIO-ECONOMIC GROUP THAT NOW BEGAN TO SUPPORT THE NAZIS WERE THE PEASANTS.

THE NAZIS HAD A VERY SUCCESSFUL CAMPAIGN IN THE RURAL AREAS, AND INFILTRATED EXISTING AGRARIAN ORGANIZATIONS.

The Nazi share of the rural vote rose from 23% in 1930 to 52% in 1933.
Their share of the vote in the towns and cities was never higher than about 40% because most workers went with the Communists.

STEPS TO POWER

HOW DID CORPORAL HITLER, THIS ONE-TIME LOSER FROM AUSTRIA, MANAGE TO RISE TO SUPREME POWER IN GERMANY?
Perfectly legally!
It never seems to happen that way when communists come to power..

MOST GERMAN CAPITALISTS AND LANDOWNERS ORIGINALLY SUPPORTED BRÜNING'S CONSERVATIVE EXPERIMENT. HOWEVER, AS THE MAJORITY OF THE WORKING AND MIDDLE CLASSES TURNED AGAINST BRÜNING, MORE OF THE GREAT CAPITALISTS AND LANDOWNERS DECLARED THEMSELVES IN FAVOR OF HIS OPPONENTS, IN OTHER WORDS, HITLER AND HUGENBERG.

...AND THE TIME WAS COMING WHEN HINDENBURG AND THE GENERALS AROUND HIM WOULD DROP BRÜNING AND ACCEPT HUGENBERG AND HITLER.

I really don't like Hitler as a person, the little Bohemian corporal who can't stop talking. But I'm not a democrat and would like an anti-democratic government in power.

PRESIDENT HINDENBURG DISLIKED HUGENBERG AND DESPISED HITLER.

DESPITE HIS NEGATIVE PERSONAL FEELINGS TOWARDS THEM, THOUGH, IN THE END HE ALLOWED THE RIGHT-WING FORCES THEY REPRESENTED TO COME TO POWER IN GERMANY.

IN FEBRUARY 1932, HITLER APPLIED FOR - AND WAS GRANTED - GERMAN CITIZENSHIP. NOW HE COULD RUN AS A CANDIDATE IN THE UPCOMING MARCH 1932 PRESIDENTIAL ELECTION AGAINST PRESIDENT HINDENBURG, WHO WANTED ANOTHER SEVEN YEARS.

Wasn't Hindenburg very old and showing signs of senility? Didn't he realize he wasn't fit for the job of President anymore?
Nope.

HITLER DIDN'T EXPECT TO BEAT HINDENBURG, WHO RAN FOR A COALITION OF PARTIES OF THE POLITICAL CENTER. WHAT HE WANTED WAS TO INCREASE HIS FOLLOWING.

SO HE CHARTERED A PLANE FROM **LUFTHANSA** TO BE ABLE TO SPEAK AT THREE OR FOUR MASS MEETINGS A DAY IN VARIOUS AREAS OF GERMANY.

AS EXPECTED, HITLER LOST THE ELECTION, BUT NAZI VOTES ROSE TO OVER THIRTEEN MILLION.

NOW THE PARTIES THAT HAD BACKED HINDENBURG DEMANDED THAT HITLER BE STOPPED ONCE AND FOR ALL.

Franz Von Papen

SO CHANCELLOR BRÜNING BANNED THE NAZI PARTY'S STORMTROOPERS, THE S.A...

...BUT THIS DIDN'T DIDN'T LAST LONG, BECAUSE IN MAY 1932, BRÜNING WAS FORCED TO RESIGN. HIS FAILURE TO EASE THE ECONOMIC DEPRESSION AND ACHIEVE POLITICAL STABILITY LED PRESIDENT HINDENBURG TO REPLACE HIM WITH **FRANZ VON PAPEN.**

This move of appointing Franz von Papen Chancellor killed the Weimar Republic.
GERMAN DEMOCRAT
VON PAPEN BEARS A LOT OF RESPONSIBILITY FOR THE ARRIVAL OF THE NAZIS TO POWER.
WHY?
BECAUSE IN JUNE 1932 HE LIFTED BRUNING'S BAN ON THE NAZI STORMTROOPERS.
GUESS WHAT HAPPENED NEXT.......
Lots of vicious street fights between the Nazi Brown-shirts and Communists! They used knives, rocks and steel pipes against each other.
PEOPLE DIED...

ONE NAZI KILLED BY THE COMMUNISTS WAS A MAN CALLED **HORST WESSEL**.

HE'D WRITTEN A MARCHING SONG, "*DIE FAHNE HOCH*" ("RAISE HIGH THE FLAG"), BEFORE HE WAS KILLED. THE NAZI PROPAGANDA MACHINE RENAMED THE POPULAR SONG "*HORST WESSEL*".

We ought to've hit the Nazi snake much earlier, *before* it got so strong.
GERMAN COMMUNIST

CHANCELLOR VON PAPEN THOUGHT HE COULD CONTROL ADOLF HITLER.

HE EVEN PROPOSED AN ELECTORAL ALLIANCE WITH HITLER AS JUNIOR PARTNER. HE DIDN'T KNOW WHOM HE WAS DEALING WITH.

We'll make Hitler do as we please.
Hmm, easier said than done.

HITLER REFUSED TO ACCEPT ANY POSITION LOWER THAN THAT OF CHANCELLOR.
Yeah, how would Hitler square being number two in the government with his *Führerprinzip*?

What did Brüning expect? People like Hitler never play second fiddle to anyone.

LIKE BRÜNING BEFORE HIM, VON PAPEN MADE THE MISTAKE OF HOLDING NEW ELECTIONS, IN JULY 1932. HITLER'S NAZI PARTY GOT NEARLY 14 MILLION VOTES (37 PERCENT OF THE TOTAL) AND 230 SEATS IN PARLIAMENT. FOR THE FIRST TIME, THE N.S.D.A.P WAS THE LARGEST PARTY IN THE *REICHSTAG*. STILL, IT DIDN'T HAVE A MAJORITY, SO NEW ELECTIONS WERE HELD IN NOVEMBER. THIS TIME THE NAZIS GOT 2 MILLION FEWER VOTES, OR 33 PERCENT OF THE TOTAL.

WHEN VON PAPEN RESIGNED ON JANUARY 28, 1933, THE ONLY ALTERNATIVE HINDENBURG HAD TO HITLER AS CHANCELLOR OF GERMANY WAS HIS ADVISER, **GENERAL KURT VON SCHLEICHER.**

HERE HE IS, ON THE LEFT. ⟹

HINDENBURG APPOINTED GENERAL **KURT VON SCHLEICHER** *REICHSKANZLER* ON DECEMBER 3, 1933.

SCHLEICHER HAD RISEN IN THE RANKS OF THE ARMY IN AN ATMOSPHERE OF SEMI-OBSCURITY AND INTRIGUE.

I have a bold plan to build a majority in the *Reichstag*.
SCHLEICHER WANTED TO UNITE THE TRADE UNIONIST LEFT WINGS IN THE VARIOUS PARTIES, INCLUDING THAT OF THE NAZIS LED BY GREGOR STRASSER.
General Schleicher

General Schleicher tried to play the part of a *"socialist general"* and entered into relations with the Christian trade unions, the left-wing members of the Nazi party, even with the Social Democrats.

SCHLEICHER PLANNED FOR A SORT OF LABOR GOVERNMENT UNDER HIS LEADERSHIP. HE PLANNED WRONG. THE *ARMY* OFFICERS WEREN'T PREPARED FOR SUCH A GOVERNMENT, AND THE WORKING CLASS HAD A NATURAL DISTRUST OF MILITARY MEN. SCHLEICHER'S IDEA DIDN'T FLY.

HAVING FAILED TO CREATE A MAJORITY GOVERNMENT, GENERAL SCHLEICHER LASTED JUST TWO MONTHS.

NOW HINDENBURG HAD TO PUT ASIDE HIS PERSONAL AND SOCIAL DISLIKE OF HITLER...
But couldn't Hindenburg have said **no** to Hitler, and looked for someone else to be Chancellor?
He feared that if he didn't accept Hitler there'd be political chaos, maybe even civil war.

PRESIDENT HINDENBURG MADE ADOLPH HITLER CHANCELLOR OF GERMANY ON JANUARY 30, 1933.

SO HITLER AND HIS NAZIS, WHO'D ALWAYS PRETENDED TO BE A REVOLUTIONARY PARTY, CAME TO POWER PERFECTLY LEGALLY. MANY HISTORIANS HAVE BEMOANED THE FACT THAT THE WOLF WAS ALLOWED INTO THE PEN BY THE DEMOCRATIC SYSTEM HE WAS ABOUT TO DESTROY. WHILE THIS IS TRUE, IT IS ALSO UNDENIABLE THAT HITLER HAD THE LARGEST PARTY IN THE *REICHSTAG*...SO HIS CHOICE BY PRESIDENT HINDENBURG WAS (UNFORTUNATELY) A LOGICAL ONE.

Adolf Hitler on January 30, 1933

NAZI STORMTROOPERS HELD A SEVEN-HOUR TORCH-LIT PARADE IN THE STREETS OF BERLIN TO CELEBRATE THEIR LEADER'S HAVING BECOME THE CHANCELLOR OF GERMANY.

THIS IS PROBABLY A GOOD PLACE TO WRITE....

...THE END

...OOPS, NOT EXACTLY....

...WELL, ALMOST. YOU DON'T HAVE TO READ THE LIST BELOW OF BOOKS ON THE WEIMAR REPUBLIC AND THE RISE OF THE NAZIS. READ IT LATER (IF YOU REALLY WANT TO). RIGHT NOW, TAKE A BREAK AND PAT YOURSELF ON THE BACK FOR HAVING FINISHED THE SECOND VOLUME OF **HMS SERIES** ON GERMANY!

Tips for further reading

THE LITERATURE ON THE WEIMAR REPUBLIC AND THE RISE OF THE NAZIS IS EXTENSIVE. THE FOLLOWING LIST CONTAINS ONLY A SMALL FRACTION OF ALL THE BOOKS WRITTEN ON THE SUBJECT IN ENGLISH. I'VE PUT IT TOGETHER FOR NON-EXPERTS ON THE BASIS OF READABILITY AND AVAILABILITY.

Abraham, David. *The Collapse of the Weimar Republic: Political Economy and Crisis*. New York, 1986.

Berghahn, V. R. *Modern Germany.* Cambridge, 1982

Bessel, Richard. *Germany after the First World War.* Oxford & New York, 1988.

Bookbinder, Paul. *Weimar Germany: the Republic of the Reasonable.* Manchester, 1996.

Broszat, Martin. *Hitler and the Collapse of Weimar Germany.* New York, 1987.

Broue, Pierre. *The German Revolution, 1917-1923*, Haymarket Books, 2006.

Childers, Thomas. *The Nazi Voter: The Social Foundations of Fascism, 1919-1933.* Chapel Hill, 1983.

Craig, Gordon A. *Germany 1866-194.* Oxford, 1980.

Eley, Geoff, ed. *Society, Culture, and the State in Germany 1870-1930.* Ann Arbor, 1997.

Evans, Richard J., The Coming of the Third Reich: How the Nazis Destroyed Democracy and Seized Power in Germany. London, 2004.

Feuchtwanter, Edgar. *From Weimar to Hitler: Germany, 1918-1933.* London, 1993.

Fritzsche, Peter. *Germans into Nazis.* Cambridge, 1998.

Fischer, Conan. *The Rise of the Nazis.* New York, 2002.

Fulbrook, Mary. *A Concise History of Germany.* Cambridge, 1994.

Fulbrook, Mary. *The Divided Nation: A History of Germany 1918-1990.* Oxford, 1991.

Hant, Claus. *Young Hitler.* London, 2010.

Harris, Nathaniel. *The Rise of Hitler.* London, 2005.

Heiber, Helmut. *The Weimar Republic.* Cambridge, Mass. 1993.

Heiden, Konrad, *The Fuhrer: Hitler's Rise to Power.* New York, 1999.

Henig, Ruth, *The Weimar Republic.* London & New York, 1998.

Herf, Jeffrey. *Reactionary Modernism: Technology, Culture and Politics in Weimar and the Third Reich.* Cambridge, 1984.

Kaes, Anton, Martin Jay, Dimendberg Edward, eds. *The Weimar Republic Sourcebook.* Berkeley, 1995.

Kershaw, Ian. *Hitler 1889-1936: Hubris.* London, 1998.

Kershaw, Ian, ed. Weimar: *Why Did German Democracy Fail?* New York, 1990.

Kolb, Eberhard. *The Weimar Republic.* New York, 2005.

McDonough, Frank, *Hitler and the Rise of the Nazi Party.* London, 2003.

McElligott, Anthony. *The German Urban Experience 1900-1945: Modernity and Crisis.* London & New York, 2001.

McElligott, Anthony, ed. *Weimar Germany* (2009).

Mommsen, Hans. *From Weimar to Auschwitz.* Princeton, 1991.

Mommsen, Hans. *The Rise and Fall of Weimar Democracy.* Chapel Hill, 1996.
Nicholls, Anthony James. *Weimar and The Rise Of Hitler.* New York, 2000.
Orlow, Dietrich. *A History of Modern Germany: 1871 to Present.* Boston, 2002.
Rosenberg, Arthur. *A History of the German Republic.* London, 1936.
Rosenhaft, Eve. *Beating the Fascists? The German Communists and Political Violence, 1929-1933.* Cambridge & New York, 1983.
Roth, Joseph. *What I Saw: Reports from Berlin 1920-1933.* New York, 2003.
Smaldone, William. *Confronting Hitler: German Social Democrats in Defense of the Weimcr Republic, 1929-1933.* Lanham MD, 2010.
Turner, Henry Ashby. *German Big Business and the Rise of Hitler.* New York, 1985.
Von Saldern, Adelheid. *The Challenge of Modernity: German Cultural Studies, 1890-1960.* Ann Arbor, 2002.
Watt, Richard. The Kings Depart: The Tragedy of Germany, Simon and Schuster, 1981.
Weitz, Eric D. *Weimar Germany: Promise and Tragedy.* Princeton, 2007.

About the Author

Kurt E. Breitner received his B.A. at Tufts University and his Ph.D. at Columbia. He has taught history at the college and high school levels in North America and Europe. His scholarly articles have appeared in academic journals in the United States, Canada, Europe and Russia.

Printed in Great Britain
by Amazon

19043801R00129